Educator's Discipline Handbook

EDUCATOR'S DISCIPLINE HANDBOOK

Robert D. Ramsey

PARKER PUBLISHING COMPANY, INC.
WEST NYACK, NEW YORK

Library of Congress Cataloging in Publication Data

Ramsey, Robert D.
    Educator's discipline handbook.

    Bibliography: p.
    Includes index.
    1.—School discipline–Handbooks, manuals,
    etc.
    I.—Title.
LB3012.R35   371.5   81-38402
ISBN 0-13-240788-4   AACR2

Printed in the United States of America

Dedication

To my wife and lifemate, Joyce.
Through the art of disciplined love,
we've built a history together.

What This Discipline Handbook Offers

EDUCATOR'S DISCIPLINE HANDBOOK offers you, for the first time, a refreshing "holistic" approach to positive school discipline through countless real-world examples that are working in school districts throughout the country. This unique resource provides you with detailed descriptions of the most successful discipline practices and procedures gathered from scores of schools across the nation.

Below are just a few of the many school-tested techniques for handling everyday discipline problems, contributed by practicing professionals from coast to coast, which appear throughout the book:

Rules of Respect—Weedsport, NY (See Chapter 1, page 25)

Dos and Don'ts for Teachers—Oxnard, CA (See Chapter 1, page 34)

Student Attendance Policy—Ligonier Valley, PA (See Chapter 2, page 54)

Bomb Threat Checklist—Grand Rapids, MI (See Chapter 2, page 77)

Bus Incident Report Form—Prior Lake, MN (See Chapter 3, page 95)

Student Records Policy—Topeka, KS (See Chapter 5, page 139)

Corporal Punishment Policy—Hillsboro, OR (See Chapter 5, page 144)

Student Grievance Procedure—Albuquerque, NM (See Chapter 6, page 177)

Suggestions for Hearing Officer Selection—Osseo, MN (See Chapter 6, page 160)

Form for Notice of Short-Term Suspension—Edmonds School District, Lynwood, WA (See Chapter 6, page 161)

Policy on Advisory Committees—Westwood Community Schools, Omaha, NB (See Chapter 7, page 199)

Five Alternative Schools—New Orleans, LA (See Chapter 8, page 217)

This unique handbook is designed as a practical, no-nonsense guide for front-line educators everywhere in defusing the "discipline bomb" found ticking in many of today's schools. Its purpose is to serve administrators and teachers as the most comprehensive, detailed "how-to" manual available for dealing with behavior problems of all kinds.

Educator's Discipline Handbook goes far beyond the traditional philosophical text on discipline. Its down-to-earth approach offers a multitude of tested, step-by-step strategies for:

• Establishing an overall positive and productive climate within the school.

• Handling the nitty-gritty nuisance problems of student behavior on a daily basis.

The handbook deals simply and directly with all dimensions of the discipline dilemma from littering to litigation. Workable procedures are spelled out for handling the school's most common "behavior bugaboos" (e.g., smoking, drugs, truancy, stealing, bomb threats), and for controlling such volatile areas as the cafeteria, playground, parking lots, school buses, and athletic fields. Additional aids are provided for curbing serious and sensitive incidences of violence and vandalism. Also included is an unprecedented special section on teenage pregnancy and VD.

Other key features of the book include:

100 Tested Discipline Tips for Teachers

Checklist for Curbing Violence

Sample Discipline Policies That Work

A Dozen Discipline Principles for Principals

How to Assure Support Through the "Parent Team" Concept

Sample Action Plans for Elementary and Secondary Schools

What You Should Know About Lawsuits

Successful Ways to Handle Corporal Punishment

Profile of the Discipline-Free Teacher

Anti-Vandalism Action Steps

How to Stay Within the Legal Limits of Proper Disciplinary Action

Schools That Have Made a Difference in Discipline

Examples of Successful Dropout Prevention Programs

Best of all, throughout the text, school personnel at all levels will find limitless examples of specific techniques for improving individual student behavior and school discipline in general; techniques which have proved effective in successful schools from all corners of the country. Through this collection, teachers and administrators alike will find *real help in solving the real problems* of improving discipline and restoring dignity and purpose to the nation's schools.

Robert D. Ramsey

Acknowledgements

Every professional work reflects the influence of countless individuals and sources. For this book, I want to particularly acknowledge the special and specific contributions of the following:

- Julie Nelson — For tenacious and talented preparation of the manuscript.

- Kimberly Ramsey — For capturing the author's unlikely likeness on film.

I am also indebted to a network of professional colleagues who are dedicated to disciplined education and who provided many of the policies, practices, and procedures featured throughout this handbook. The members of this network are identified in Chapter 10.

R.D.R.

TABLE OF CONTENTS

CHAPTER 6
Steps to Establishing Effective
Discipline Policies 151

CHAPTER 7
Using Parents as Partners for Positive
Discipline. 179

1

Blueprint
for Better Behavior
in Your School

Wherever people congregate to talk about schools and schooling, the number one topic of conversation is *discipline*. Talking about unruly students has always been a popular pastime, but today's discipline discussions have taken on a new sense of urgency and reflect a sharper edge of concern.

Discipline in the 1980's is different than ever before. Students are more outspoken, animated, and aggressively protective of their rights than in previous years. Parents reflect a new brand of assertiveness and skepticism of the school's control. Communities contain an increasingly diverse mixture of values and expectations for school authorities. In addition, the tools of disruption available to students are dramatically more plentiful and potentially more dangerous than in any other time in the history of public education.

In these kinds of trying times, there are many emergency measures and first-aid formulas that professionals can impose to establish temporary serenity and stability in an explosive school situation. But, ultimately it is the eros of the school—its character and disposition—that determines whether or not an enduring pattern of positive behavior will prevail.

Regardless of the nature of the community or the type of student served, the discipline tone of the school is the creation of the school staff. For good or ill, the attitudinal atmosphere is

almost exclusively attributable to teacher and administrator behavior. Despite whatever unfavorable forces may exist outside the
school, the staff can make a difference and can make a climate
conducive to effective learning.

This chapter pinpoints those elements that are necessary in
any school to make it an interesting, safe, and supportive place for
young people to be and to grow. The suggestions that follow lay
the groundwork on which teachers and administrators can build
an ongoing action plan for fostering positive pupil behavior.

HOW TO AVOID A SUREFIRE RECIPE
FOR UNREST IN YOUR SCHOOL

Where discipline is the worst, fingerpointing, accusations,
and blame-laying abound. Almost without exception in these
instances, the school itself is an integral part of the problem.

It is easy to develop a discipline nightmare in any school. The
few necessary ingredients include:

- A blend of negative expectations and pessimism regarding
  students. (The best indicator of these factors is the tenor of
  talk in the teachers' lounge. If staff conversations focus on
  complaints about how terrible students are and dire predic-
  tions for their future, the school is in trouble.)
- An attitude that there is nothing wrong with the school—
  there is merely an influx of inferior students.
- An autocratic administration committed to securing un-
  questioned acquiescence and order at all costs.
- A bankrupt philosophy of discipline based on fear, intimidation, coercion, and the power of punishment.
- A willingness to permit street ethics to become the accepted
  code of behavior within the school.
- A blatant disregard for student rights.
- A large measure of inattention and insensitivity to ethnic or
  racial concerns.
- A strong sense of student alienation and isolation within the
  school.
- An absence of student involvement and input in any
  significant decision-making process.

- A generous scorn for parent and community involvement (separation of the school and the home).

- An explosion of rules and an obsession with formalized procedures.

- A rich mixture of highly structured curriculum tracks. (Excessive tracking tends to limit peer interaction by producing separate student subcultures, whereby low-esteem students and high-esteem students rarely mix.)

- A narrow, rigid curriculum that stresses content at all costs and knowledge first—feelings later.

- A subtle "silent curriculum" that conveys in a variety of nonverbal ways that students are not to be trusted or respected. (Each teacher shares the responsibility for serving as sentinel of the silent curriculum, and as such, has some ownership over the kinds of nonverbal messages that students receive from the school.)

- An uninspired and insipid activity program.

- An uncompromising reward system that recognizes only a very narrow band of success.

- A rigid, unrealistic, and sometimes punitive grading policy.

- A heavy emphasis on competition in every facet of school activity.

- A drab physical environment.

- A conscious effort to limit pupil access to teachers and administration.

- A stifling commitment to preserve the status quo.

Any substantial combination of these factors will guarantee a discipline disaster in any school. Unfortunately, some school staffs seem determined to be their own worst enemies by clinging to such counterproductive measures despite dramatic changes in time and circumstances. The psychology of this kind of self-defeating school is summed up in the following statement by M. Donald Thomas (Superintendent, Salt Lake City Schools):

The truth of the discipline matter is simple. Everyone has given up. Teachers hide in their classrooms and eat lunch there and won't go out in the halls to do any supervising. Principals don't want to get involved either. Scapegoating is practiced by every member of the education community.

To avoid almost certain collapse of control and/or to turn around a school "gone sour," teachers and principals must root out or reverse any of the elements described above that exist in their school.

In contrast to these sure-fired ingredients for failure, the next section spells out conditions that must be built in to the school milieu to assure a minimum problem environment. This section also presents specific examples of successful *climate control* practices currently at work in a sampling of school districts.

MAXIMIZING POSITIVE BEHAVIOR
THROUGH CLIMATE CONTROL

Beyond question, the *prevention dimension* is the most critical component of the school's efforts to provide a disciplined arena for effective teaching and learning. Without a prevailing mood of cooperation and human concern, interfaced with visible evidence of support and respect, no arsenal of remedial measures will result in a stable discipline environment.

Successful schools result from the staff that takes specific overt action to structure a positive atmosphere. Most of the factors that make up the overall climate of the school are within the control of the professional staff. What teachers and administrators think and do dictates in large measure how students will behave.

The superstructure of a well-disciplined school is built upon a positive Pygmalian perspective. The school is an embodiment of the staff's self-fulfilling prophecy. What teachers and principals expect is largely what they get in terms of student actions and attitudes. To control the school's environment positively, the staff must maintain positive expectations for student performance and behavior. Every aspect of the school's operation should reflect that the faculty expects success, assumes individual human worth, and firmly believes that most students will respond favorably to good teaching and fair discipline.

The goal of the school should be to establish a feeling of family within the learning community. This means that the staff must value an environment characterized by *trust, sharing, caring,* and *excitement.* To achieve this form of family environment, all of the school's policies and programs should somehow be directly related to the three fundamental needs of the student body:

a. Safety

b. Self-actualization/fulfillment

c. Esteem

Item number three is crucial. Positive, productive behavior (in and out of the classroom) depends heavily on student self-esteem.

In designing a school climate that is both controlled and constructive, the five guiding principles for effective discipline outlined below can serve as practical benchmarks for the school personnel.

---

*FIVE FUNDAMENTAL GUIDING PRINCIPLES

Harold L. Hula
Washburn University, Topeka, Kansas

1. ...the most important factors in the development and maintenance of good discipline within a school lie in the *attitude and effort of the entire school staff.*

2. ...*the welfare of the student is of primary importance.* The focus of good discipline should be on helping the student in his adjustment and development in the school.

3. ...*(all of) the staff members who have significant contact with the student and the parents should be involved in the disciplinary process.*

4. ...*young people need an atmosphere of structure.* They need to know the rules of the game and they need to know that the rules are enforced. Limitations and controls within the school are not only necessary for the smooth functioning of a school, but they are desirable and, in fact, essential for a student's personal development.

5. ...those who are involved with the student and who participate in the discipline process need to have a *positive attitude toward the student and a recognition of the goals of discipline.*

---

*Ramsey, Henson, and Hula. *The Schools Within a School Program: A Modern Approach to Secondary Instruction and Guidance* (West Nyack, NY: Parker Publishing Co., 1967), pp. 152-158.

As part of its R_x for a healthy climate, the school should consider adding the following important elements:

- Strategies for the early identification of and early intervention with "stifled" students (students who are isolated, uninvolved, or merely adrift in the school).

- A governing system that accentuates accessibility to all teachers and administrators.

- Systems for ensuring that every student is known by some responsible staff member. No school should become so crowded that there is no room for individual student identity.

- Opportunities for successful rebellion. There should always be some escape mechanism that permits fledgling citizens to spread their wings, alter some conditions, and influence certain outcomes.

- An orientation toward producing self-induced conduct control.

- An emphasis on productivity and satisfaction for teachers and learners alike.

- Provision for recognizing both students and staff who accomplish things of interest and benefit. Such recognition should be widespread throughout the school and not restricted to a limited number of "leaders."

- Options for modifying and extending the school environment to include appropriate learning posts throughout the community. (Through community based action learning programs, the school can redefine its custodial role and become more than a single locus of learning. This broadening approach tends to minimize inhibiting restrictions that engender negative actions and reactions by students.)

All of these factors contribute to a vital climate that produces good feelings, good attitudes, and good discipline, while limiting anti-social, anti-school behavior.

The examples that follow illustrate practical applications of effective climate-control programs selected from a variety of present-day schools:

1. *Stillwater (MN) Junior High*—The discipline approach at Stillwater is based on creating a trusting atmosphere where

teachers are humane to students and students feel they have a stake in their school. To this end, the Stillwater program features:

a. An early intervention discipline procedure (parents are contacted immediately when problems are first noticed).

b. A program of student government (patterned after the national political system) whereby the Student Council serves as a real power structure for students.

c. A *behavior management graphing* system in which student conduct in five areas (e.g., attitude, promptness, etc.), is charted all day long by teachers, parents, counselors, and even custodians. This graphing is designed to give the student a clear picture of behavior problems and a sense that change is possible.

2. *Weedsport (NY) Junior-Senior High School*—The Weedsport staff underscores the kind of climate desired in the school by promulgating, distributing, and widely discussing the Rules of Respect that follow.

RULES OF RESPECT

Weedsport Central School, Weedsport, NY

The school staff finds that in order to provide an acceptable quality of education for students it is necessary that *all* students show appropriate cooperation and respect toward faculty, substitute teachers, and staff members. Lack of cooperation and disrespect, more than any other factors, interfere with our ability to provide students with satisfactory learning experiences.

With these ideas in mind we will direct particular concern to the following rules of good conduct. These are not new rules but old rules newly emphasized for students in grades six through twelve.

Language

It is expected that language directed toward staff members and fellow students will be polite and appropriate. Profanity, obscenity, and vulgarity have no place in the school setting. This pertains not only to students as individuals but also as a part of larger groups. Yelling offensive chants in the cafeteria or at athletic events is as inappropriate as if you were saying these words as an individual.

Similarly, offensive wording or pictures on T-shirts or other clothing are considered another inappropriate use of language.

Following Directions

Directions by teachers, substitutes, and other members of the school staff must be followed. You as a student may not always agree with the directions of a staff member but the staff member has a position of authority that must be respected. Students have recourse in situations where they feel inappropriately directed, but they do not have the right to refuse the directions as given.

Consequences

Students reaching grade six and throughout junior-senior high school should be aware that there are consequences for their actions, both good and bad. The consequences of good conduct include the establishment of a good reputation among staff members (one that might someday help you attain a job, receive a recognition, etc.), and equally as important, the opportunity to become an educated person. Consequences of bad behavior, whether as an individual or as a member of a group, vary with the "degree of offense." Parent conferences, suspensions, and permanent expulsions from school are not considered too severe measures for the school to take in order to maintain an atmosphere conducive to good education.

Our expectations for student behavior are realistic. They are the minimums that well-mannered ladies and gentlemen of any age may be expected to use at all times. We expect nothing more; we will accept nothing less.

3. *Hillcrest Elementary School*—Like many effective schools throughout the country, the Hillcrest School (Bloomington, MN) has built its climate control program around the techniques of Reality Therapy as developed by Dr. William Glasser.* Over a period of years, the entire Hillcrest staff has been trained in Glasser's strategies and has implemented a comprehensive program designed to help children verbalize and evaluate misbehavior, make specific plans for improvement, and secure commitment to positive change.

*Glasser, Dr. William. *Reality Therapy.* (New York: Harper and Row & Co., 1972).

The Hillcrest plan focuses on strengthening pupil self-concepts through a caring relationship (concern-love) involving students, teachers, and the principal. A variety of self-esteem activities (e.g., class meetings) are conducted to enhance pupil self-images and positive interrelationships. The responsibility for developing a school atmosphere that helps students assume responsibility for their own behavior rests with *all* who come in contact with them.

4. *Pleasant View (IA) Elementary School*—As part of a total schoolwide climate-building effort (Project "R") described in Chapter 8 of this handbook, Pleasant View personnel have inaugurated a successful, systematic positive reinforcement program utilizing the simple procedure below.

SCHOOL-WIDE PROCEDURE
FOR POSITIVE REINFORCEMENT

• Each full-time teacher on the school staff will send at least twenty positive notes (happy grams, notes, etc.) home with deserving students each month and make at least four personal contacts with parents to report something positive.

• Part-time teachers will send home ten positive notes and make two personal contacts with parents each month to report something positive.

---

5. *Montevideo (MN) Middle School*—As a different approach to dealing with the uniqueness of individual students, an effective teacher/advisor program was introduced by the Montevideo Middle School Staff in 1971.

Several aspects of the Montevideo model outlined below are held in common with similar programs in a number of states:

a. All teachers are assigned 15 to 20 students as advisees.

b. School time is used for group meetings.

c. The advisor serves as a kind of parent-at-school.

The theme of the Montevideo program is "to humanize, to individualize, and to have (a school) where caring is a personal relationship."

A partial list of goals for the Montevideo program includes:

- promoting and providing for communication among students of different grades
- helping the student develop an appreciation for the school community
- helping the individual recognize his or her own worth and responsibility
- being used as a means of communication between the school and the home
- using the parent-student-advisor conference model to gather and share information with parents

6. *Heim Middle School (Williamsburg, NY)*—As a graphic testimony to the kind of climate stressed at the Heim Middle School, the student handbook features the following admonishment:

HEIM MIDDLE SCHOOL

Happiness is...

....taking part in school sponsored activities, such as the Student Council and intramurals

....being a part of Student Council election campaigns

....helping one another

....passing all my subjects

....participating in the school picnic in June

....going to school sponsored dances

....helping to collect old clothes and food for poor people

....helping to keep our school neat and clean

....attending assemblies

....being a student in Heim Middle School

....working hard

....learning

All of the ideas and illustrations above can provide educators with the tools for defining a school climate that maximizes student potential and positive discipline. The most important quality of such an environment must be a solid pattern of two-way communication between the adults and the young people who make up the school community. The next section offers additional tips for alleviating communication blockages and freeing adult-child relationships.

SOLVING COMMUNICATION PROBLEMS THROUGH INPUT AND INVOLVEMENT

The centerpiece of the school's program for maintaining a mellow behavioral atmosphere must be positive, free, and frequent communication among all parties involved. Students must have not only meaningful opportunities to express themselves, but they must also *believe* that they are really heard. (They don't necessarily expect tangible action in response to every request or complaint.)

Sooner or later, communication problems become discipline problems. To avoid both, many schools find the techniques listed below workable and worthwhile:

- A school cabinet comprised of students and faculty to deal with touchy issues in the school.
- An effective, simple student grievance procedure.
- A periodic open forum on school rules conducted by the principal.
- Elected student advisor(s) to the school board (pupils granted formal ex-officio status on the board to represent the views of the student body).
- A committee on student behavior, comprised of students, teachers, administrators, and parents.
- A student council with clout.
- "Orchids and Onions" notes to the principal that provide an open opportunity for student suggestions and comments on any issue.
- Student representation on important district committees (e.g., Curriculum Advisory Council, Long-Range Planning Committee, etc.).

- A viable student newspaper that permits the free expression of opinion as long as legal requirements and the standards of ethical journalism are satisfied.
- Student ombudspersons in the school (some districts successfully use CETA employees in this role).
- Student evaluation of teachers.

Any measures such as the above that encourage responsible student input and involvement help tip the scales in favor of better behavior and decrease the likelihood of discipline eruptions.

There are always a few students, however, who seem to defy the best efforts of the school and remain almost unreachable. The next section pinpoints some specific clues for recognizing these students.

WAYS TO SPOT POTENTIAL PROBLEM STUDENTS
—THE FACE OF THE OFFENDER

An important addition to the school's kit of *climate control* measures should be a definite plan for early identification and intervention in problem situations. An ounce of anticipation and early intervention is worth a pound of punishment after problems arise. Successful teachers and administrators seem to develop a special antenna for spotting potential trouble and troublemakers.

Bias should never be the basis for prejudice or prejudgment of any child; remember, not all problems are recognizable in their early stages. Yet despite the lack of foolproof warning signs or danger signals, there are certain psycho-socio characteristics common to many problem-prone students. Every member of the school staff should be alert to these symptoms.

In most schools, the vast majority of discipline offenders are males. (This may be the harvest of a long history of sexual stereotyping.) The most explosive and volatile ages seem to be between 12-17. A disproportionately high number of discipline problems often come from families living in apartments and public housing. At the core of many potential offenders is a deeply imbedded sense of "no future." These students are often characterized by an attitude of defeatism and pessimism. They typically believe that everyone starts out with an "F" in school and in life and has to work against odds to get a "D." They often view the school as alien to their values. Since they do not expect to go on to college, they tend to believe that school (particularly high school) is unimportant. They are frequently supersensitive and defensive and become rebellious when dealt with in an autocratic manner. Students who match this composite portrait are all too often discipline problems looking for a place to happen. Unfortunately, too many students in this nation match this unhappy description.

Figure 1-1 further depicts the psycho-socio traits and forces commonly found at work in the most serious school discipline cases.

Obviously, not all problem students fit this profile. Any student can be (and at sometime is) a discipline problem in disguise. Even the smiling face of the most well-scrubbed cherub can mask mayhem in the making. Nevertheless, the school staff is well-advised to pay particular attention early on to pupils who embody the discipline indicators identified in Figure 1-1. When such potential problem students are recognized, the challenge to the teacher and the administrator is not to *expect* less, but to *care* more.

Just as there are certain traits that typify the most common problem students, there are identifiable qualities that characterize those teachers who, year in and year out, have almost no discipline problems in their classes. Every school has at least a few such teachers. These are the kind of productive professionals that every teacher strives to become and that every principal strives to have on his or her staff. The following is an in-depth look at the kind of teacher who makes good discipline happen.

PROFILE OF THE DISCIPLINE-FREE TEACHER

Some teachers seem to come by good discipline naturally. Something in their makeup or in their mastery of the craft of teaching enables them almost to assure proper behavior by their mere presence. These teachers avoid the trap of *discipline fixation* whereby so much time, attention, and effort is devoted to main-

DIAGRAM OF A DISCIPLINE PROBLEM

A Composite Portrait of the Typical
Discipline Offender

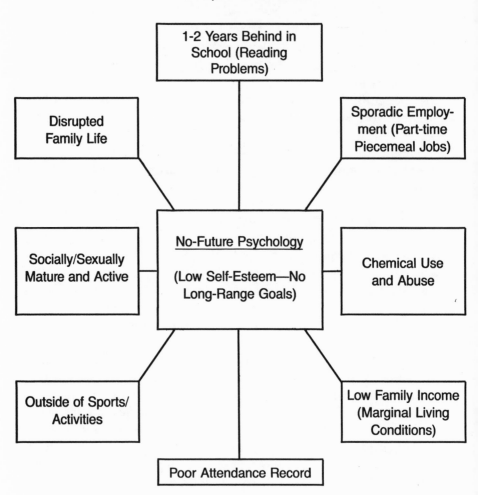

Figure 1-1

taining discipline that teaching suffers and a cycle of pyramiding problems becomes entrenched in the classroom. These teachers seldom have to think about maintaining discipline and rarely know why they are so effective.

From numerous studies of student feelings, teacher observations, and supervisors' perceptions, the following traits emerge as universal sure-signs of successful teaching.

Images of the Discipline-Free Teacher

- Holds a positive self-image (an attitude of "I'm enough").
- Radiates confidence.
- Remains ever optimistic.
- Believes that students are basically good and can succeed.
- Stays young (sets new and interesting self-goals).
- Avoids perfectionism.
- Is businesslike, organized, and prepared *every day.*
- Listens.
- Can recognize ridiculousness and can laugh at life and at his or herself (appreciates humor as one of the few remaining natural problem solvers).
- Is open and consistent.
- Maintains absolute honesty.
- Possesses capacity to put his or herself on a feeling level with others (what existentialists call the quality of *Dasien*—of "being there" with another person).
- Is surgent (avoids dullness).
- Reflects warmth and affection.
- Lets student know he or she cares (makes students aware of his or her awareness of them and their needs).
- Demonstrates elegance and eloquence in teaching (does common things uncommonly well).
- Is decentered.
- Maintains resiliency.
- Expresses sympathy.
- Is imaginative and creative.
- Reflects exuberance in teaching (is fresh in the classroom every morning).
- Possesses individualized style/flair for teaching (maintains a unique "batting stance" in the classroom).

The above traits mark the optimally effective teacher. These teachers will have some discipline problems, but they will never have very many and the problems will rarely be severe or longlasting.

All teachers can learn from those possessing these traits, but not all teachers can internalize these qualities to the extent that they will be relatively discipline free themselves. It is possible, however, for most teachers to achieve adequacy in teaching and to become reasonably effective in maintaining desired discipline. In fact, it is imperative that they do so. The next section offers a jam-packed collection of down-to-earth hints that can help *all* teachers improve their discipline.

100 TESTED DISCIPLINE TIPS FOR TEACHERS

The teacher represents the first line of defense against disruption in the school. If discipline is to succeed, it will succeed because of what teachers are and what they do in and out of the classroom. The importance of teachers to good discipline and good discipline to teachers is reflected in the following "Dos and Don'ts" quotation from materials developed for beginning teachers in the Oxnard, California Public Schools.

DOS AND DON'TS FOR TEACHERS

(Oxnard, CA)

Teaching might be fun if it weren't for kids.

—Anonymous

The words are those of a beginning teacher—a very frustrated beginning teacher. The identity is irrelevant. Similar laments have been uttered by teachers from New York to Oshkosh, from Los Angeles to Topeka, perhaps at one time or another in just about every school district across the country. The words decry a common problem: discipline.

And the problem is by no means reserved for beginners. Discipline is one of the most serious problems the beginning teacher faces. But, if it is any comfort to the novice, experienced teachers often find it baffling, too!

There is no point to public education unless teachers can become "unbaffled" about discipline. The problem is that (as in many professions), what works in teaching (e.g., motivating students, maintaining order, etc.), appears seductively simple, but actually is deceptively difficult. This simple-while-difficult dichotomy is evidenced in the Seven Elements for Establishing a Climate of Classroom Control.

**SEVEN ELEMENTS FOR ESTABLISHING
A CLIMATE OF CLASSROOM CONTROL**

(Good Teaching for Good Discipline)
Windom (MN) Elementary Schools

- Every child who walks in your door wants you to see him as an individual. He wants you to notice him, to accept him, to like him, and to be interested in him personally. The essence of your control, as well as your power to inspire learning, lies right here.
- Expect good behavior. Children want to measure up to your expectations, so accent the positive.
- Develop mental antennae that wave in every direction, picking up moods and feelings of the people in your room. This sensitivity comes with having complete knowledge of your children.
- Take time to check out the physical aspects of your room, temperature, adjustments of shades, and light. Never stand in front of the windows to teach, causing children to look at the light.
- Plenty of work at the correct level is an absolute essential. Will your slow learners have success today? Is there extra challenging work for your fast learners? Plan for those who finish first. Plan variety.
- Have you organized?
- Be fair.

The principles involved in these elements seem obvious and elementary, but the energy and expertise required to make them reality extracts the utmost from any professional instructor. Teaching is a tough, draining business. Society asks the teacher to be "dynamite" every day in the face of the infinite demands and endless expectations of a room full of energetic children and youth.

The task is not easy, but it is possible! Part of the trick is to achieve control before realizing exhaustion. The proven suggestions that follow have helped many teachers to improve discipline while reducing the emotional wear and tear of the classroom.

100 Tested Discipline Tips for Teachers

1. Understand that implementing positive discipline begins with the teacher's self-understanding. The teacher must feel adequate and self-accepting before a sense of security and stability can be established in the classroom.

2. Adopt a professional philosophy of preparation (being *totally* prepared), respect, and dedication. (Such a personal philosophy of commitment is a cornerstone for coping with student learning and behavior problems.)

3. Be rested (build in renewal opportunities and rewards for yourself). Students demand energy. Fatigue breeds short tempers. Tired teachers tend to be overly cautious, conservative, and restrictive because they are afraid they might not be able to handle the situation if they loosen the reins.

4. Remain steadfastly enthusiastic and courteous. (Maintain a sense of humor.)

5. Establish positive expectations. Make the concept of a self-fulfilling prophecy work for you in the classroom.

6. Establish routines. This is the initial step in securing discipline.

7. Know every student! Show you care. Be sensitive to moods. Encourage self-disclosure. The more the teacher knows about the student and the student knows about the teacher, the better the communication and the fewer the problems.

8. Do interesting things in the classroom. Be alive! Stand! Move! Alter your routine! A teaching certificate is not a license to bore. If the teacher is bored, students will be bored and act accordingly.

9. Know fully all school policies and rules.

10. Ensure that every student has been informed of all rules. Some successful teachers use their roll book to

record which students have received full instruction on policies and regulations to preclude any omissions.

11. Keep classroom rules few and simple. (The acronym, KISS—"Keep It Simple, Stupid"—should be applied to regulations within the classroom.)

12. Be fair—always. Consistency is essential.

13. Have the courage to be imperfect and to permit students the same luxury. Admit errors and apologize if necessary.

14. Be personal. Stress *you, me,* and *us.* Use names as early in the year as possible.

15. Don't be an historian. Don't prejudge students on the basis of what you know about the family, older siblings, past problems, etc. Start fresh with every student.

16. Don't take misbehavior personally. (Avoid paranoia.)

17. Avoid comparing one student with another (e.g., "Why don't you behave like Susie?")

18. Don't label students.

19. Eliminate emotion-laden blaming and threatening.

20. Don't dwell on or overreact to small imperfections or minor infractions. (Don't make the student feel that every mistake is a sin.)

21. Convey a "no nonsense" approach, as defined by William Glasser. Don't accept excuses in place of results.

22. Deal with issues and behavior—not with personalities.

23. Don't deal with discipline problems in anger. Don't allow yourself to become angry at an entire group because of the actions of a few members.

24. Don't assign homework or additional schoolwork as punishment.

25. Never humiliate a child. (This fosters peer wrath.)

26. Remember that the overuse of punishment strengthens the student's powers of resistance and defiance.

27. Fit the punishment to the offense.

28. Be friendly, but do not try to become "part of the gang." In most cases, students need a teacher, not another buddy. Avoid trying to win student affection by adopting the language of youth, emulating student dress, etc.

29. Remember that touching goes a long way in conveying that you care (at the elementary level).

30. Avoid "do it or else" situations and "no win" challenges (e.g., "the next person who _____ will _____.") Don't make threats you can't deliver.

31. Know the difference between *praise* and *encouragement* and their effects. (Praise rewards the individual and recognizes the actor. Encouragement focuses on the effort and acknowledges the action.)

32. Don't mix positive and negative comments. Confusing or contradictary messages force the child to wonder what is real.

33. Don't force public confessions of wrongdoing.

34. Don't demand explanations for all infractions. (The student may not know why he or she did it.)

35. Avoid clichés and preaching.

36. Don't nag.

37. Expect students to test your honesty.

38. Refrain from punishing when the child takes initiative to correct behavior.

39. Strive for some kind of genuine encounter with every student every day. (A mere 15 seconds a day of focused attention on each individual student can go a long way to engender respect and cooperation.)

40. Practice "active listening." Work at understanding the sender's message.

41. Anticipate that students will search out and try to exploit the teacher's weakness(es).

42. Don't maintain double standards for minorities, for one sex or the other, etc.

43. Make effective use of eye contact, voice control, body language, and distance management. The following simple techniques often work wonders:

   • use "soft" reprimands
   • face students directly
   • employ pauses
   • sit troublemakers close by (proximity control)

- move towards inattentive students (walk right up to the offending student's desk if necessary)
- lean toward students who are misbehaving
- use facial expressions to convey "I mean business"

44. Avoid the fallacy of the first impulse. (Be deliberate—maintain perspective.)

45. Don't equate teaching with entertainment (e.g., fashioning the class after TV, telling jokes, playing games, etc.). Strive for enthusiasm through interesting ideas and the joy of achievement.

46. Be willing to put up with silence so students can think.

47. Don't strong-arm students.

48. Be willing to understand and consider extenuating circumstances (e.g., provocation, experience, age, etc.).

49. Avoid open arguments with students.

50. Ensure that all criticism is specific, direct, *private*, immediate, and clear. (Have the student paraphrase if necessary.)

51. Don't use the classroom to play "oneupmanship" with other teachers or administrators (e.g., attempt to be more lenient, offer bigger and better rewards, etc.).

52. Remember that the worst thing the teacher can do is to have a rule and not enforce it.

53. Approach upset students (and upset parents) by really listening to what they have to say.

54. Be authentic. Students can always spot a phony. Don't attempt to be what you are not.

55. Make a reminder note every time you make a threat to a student.

56. Introduce some lessons in "manners education."

57. Use peer counseling as a tool for reaching troubled and troublesome students.

58. Understand that disorder expands proportionately to the tolerance for it.

59. Have at least one silly rule for students to test and let off steam about.

60. Know the real role of rules in the classroom (e.g., rules

must be consistently enforced, involve logical consequences, provide incremental punishment, and be fully understood).

61. Teach self-control skills such as:
    - anticipating consequences
    - appreciating feelings
    - managing frustration
    - learning restraints
    - relaxation techniques

62. Hold "sound off" sessions (permit students to air gripes, identify problems, discuss issues, etc.).

63. Use sustained silent reading as a mood modifier.

64. If citizenship grades are used, make sure their meaning is clear (see example):

MEANING OF CITIZENSHIP MARKS

1. The student shows outstanding cooperation and participation in classroom activities. He or she constantly exhibits mature qualities of self-control, responsibility, and respect.

2. The student usually cooperates and generally exhibits respect for others, self-control, and an acceptable amount of responsibility. (The majority of students normally will be given this mark.)

3. The student demonstrates less than desirable cooperation and does not always accept sufficient responsibility, self-control, and respect for others.

4. The student seldom cooperates in class. He or she shows a lack of maturity, responsibility, self-control, and respect for others.

---

65. Remember that there are two visions of every discipline problem: the teacher's and the student's. Get both versions by way of a private conference before taking action.

66. Understand that behavior modification cannot serve as the primary discipline technique for an entire classroom.

67. Arrange for problem students to meet weekly with a local celebrity (e.g., professional athlete) as a source of positive motivation.

68. Look for the real source of misbehavior (see below):

FOUR COMMON GOALS OF MISCONDUCT

a. Signal for attention
b. Power/influence/intimidation
c. Retaliation (vendetta)
d. Expression of inadequacy, frustration or pain

---

69. Give students a rest when pressure builds up.

70. Keep a record of the kinds of presentations and activities that foster boredom and replace them with more interesting techniques in later units.

71. Don't succumb to the temptation to make an example out of any pupil.

72. Use flip cards as reminders of classroom rules regarding noise, movement, paying attention, or interaction.

73. Make wise use of physical and verbal calming techniques (e.g., physical separation, visual separation, personal space) in tense situations.

74. Use overt teacher cues (words, looks, etc.), to initiate desired behavior(s) and then gradually reduce such cues and work toward student initiation.

75. Understand that only mediocre teachers are dependent on impersonal rules to provide a captive audience and proper behavior.

76. Provide an option for students to step out of the classroom or the school for a cooling-off period. (The student should be permitted to return without penalty or loss of status.)

77. Send disruptive students to a well-run classroom at a different grade level. (This requires advanced planning with the receiving teacher.)

78. Note on a checklist the steps taken to prevent having to refer students for disciplinary action before making any such referral. (The checklist itself serves as a reminder of possible alternatives and as a safeguard against unnecessary referrals.)

79. Remind yourself that the most unpleasant, unappealing, and unruly student you have may be the one who needs you most.

80. Don't teach in a T-formation (e.g., directing all attention and instruction to those students seated down and across the middle of the classroom).

81. Try a Tolerance Day, whereby the disruptive student is permitted to come to school as long as "you can take it."

82. Understand that actions speak louder than words in conflict situations. (Students tend to be "teacher-deaf" at these times.)

83. Arrange for other teachers or administrators to serve as advocates or personal counselors for problem students as a method of attacking discipline problems early. (This can be particularly effective if students can choose the staff member with whom they feel most comfortable.)

84. Arrange seats in a horseshoe and stand in the middle. (Teacher proximity limits inattention and misconduct.)

85. Realize that students don't rebel against adults as much as they rebel against adult oppression of their individuality and rights.

86. Provide detention alternatives (e.g., study hall, counseling session, work detail, combination of all of these).

87. Don't wait too long to engage parents in trouble situations.

88. Guard against sarcasm. (Sarcasm always alienates.)

89. In dealing with fights or arguments between students, have the pupils involved write down their explanation of the situation first, then discuss. This provides a cooling-off and calming-down process.

90. Gain insight by role-playing a variety of discipline situations with other teachers.

91. Give students punishment options that must be selected immediately, such as:
    - Take away a classroom privilege
    - Isolate student
    - Change seats for a specific period of time
    - Relinquish a few minutes of free time
    - Contact parents

92. Model appropriate behavior (e.g., refrain from talking to other teachers during assembly programs).

93. Use the physical education program to curb discipline and provide energy outlets (see examples below).

**Emotional Energy Outlets
Through Physical Education**

- Stress lifelong sports and recreation activities
- Use acting-out exercises
- Post listings of available activities and events in the community
- Set up a varied intramural program
- Provide tickets to local sporting events

---

94. Choose a student who is causing discipline problems and write down what has been done to handle the situation. Eliminate the ineffective steps. Apply with renewed vigor the measures that have worked (even if limited) and/or try new approaches.

95. Study formal/commercial classroom management programs (e.g., "Reality Therapy," Magic Circle," etc.).

96. Provide action learning (community based) opportunities for restless students.

97. Provide *daily* behavior reports to parents of special problem students (call at work if necessary).

98. Get help from fellow teachers. Break down isolation by arranging for a friend or association representative to observe the classroom.

99. Don't futurize (e.g., "You'll never amount to anything.")

100. Don't expect or attempt the impossible. No teacher bats a thousand.

If *every* teacher would follow *every* one of the tips above *every* day, any school could miraculously become a model of positive discipline in a short time.

The final component of the blueprint for better behavior rests on the quality and performance of a single individual—the building principal. The administrator in charge should be the central actor in the drama of any school (elementary or secondary) and as such, carries the ultimate burden of shaping the school's disciplinary character.

The last portion of this chapter details some of the guidelines that should be at the forefront of every principal's action plan for managing the school.

A DOZEN DISCIPLINE PRINCIPLES FOR PRINCIPALS

More than any other single person, the school principal is the key to successful discipline. Consciously and unconsciously the entire school staff mirrors the strengths, weaknesses, and priorities of the principal. It is up to the building leader to set the limits and to stick to them. The guiding principles below offer a platform for this kind of leadership:

1. The basis for discipline is effective instruction. Positive behavior is a byproduct of sound teaching.

2. Schools are not intrinsically all good or all bad. Every school and every classroom is a mix of positive and negative factors.

3. Individualized discipline is as important as individualized instruction. Fair and equal discipline does not demand that everyone receive exactly the same treatment or punishment.

4. The only way to change behavior is through feelings.

5. Nothing improves unless there is involvement on the part of staff, students, and parents.

6. Most students want to achieve, to get along with others, and to go along with reasonable rules.

7. The inappropriate actions of children and youth are largely products of how adults treat them (at home and at school).

8. Victimization is reduced in schools characterized by close teacher-principal cooperation.

9. The principal must know the law. Innocent omissions or inadvertent violations of due process can jeopardize any single disciplinary decision or action; the overall effectiveness of the school's total discipline program; and more importantly, the administrator's entire future career.

10. One teacher whose class or classroom is completely out of control can infect and affect the entire school. (The principal must exercise every means possible to maintain a subtle revolving door for incompetents and to weed out any "discipline duds" on the staff.)

11. The principal does not have to be the best teacher in the building. But the principal must know what good teaching is and have the skills necessary to help all teachers get better.

12. When caught in a cross fire of conflicting views, the principal's first choice of action should always be determined by what's best for the student (now and in the future).

This chapter sketched the skeleton of how a healthy, successful school is structured. Chapter 2 begins to flesh out the skeleton by providing some fresh, thought-provoking measures for dealing with the most persistent discipline problems that plague schools in this country.

2

New Approaches to Old Behavior Bugaboos

Some of the most relentless and reoccurring discipline problems for school officials exist in the areas of *attendance, drug use, smoking, stealing,* and *bomb threats.* Like the inevitable cycle of the seasons, these same violations reappear each year to trouble the tranquility of many schools.

A few decades ago, these offenses were most common at the secondary level and caused only minor concerns for elementary school personnel. Today, this distinction has become increasingly blurred. Administrators at all levels now testify that a malproportion of time and attention must be focused on these five trouble spots.

To achieve proper balance and businesslike behavior, the school must gain control of these persistent "bugaboos" without aggravating them. The next sections point out action-oriented alternatives for dealing successfully with these perennial problems.

EFFECTIVE WAYS OF HANDLING ATTENDANCE

Effective attendance procedures must be at the forefront of every school's discipline program. The school simply won't work if it is marred by a lack of regular attendance. Ironically, as enrollments taper off, truancy problems seem to be skyrocketing in many areas. The "student disappearing act" has become the number one headache for a growing segment of teachers and administrators. Selective attendance (skipping individual classes) is becoming an increasingly prevalent phenomenon.

The causes of increased absenteeism encompass a broad range of contributing factors such as the following:

- A dull, narrow spectrum of curriculum offerings
- Lack of interaction between students and teachers
- Ineffective classroom practices (Absenteeism is one infallible indicator of teacher ineffectiveness.)
- Apathetic teacher attitudes toward attendance
- Poor parental attitudes
- Lack of pupil success in school
- Peer pressure
- An uninviting overall school atmosphere
- A nonsupporting home environment
- Lack of interest in subject matter
- Poor attendance policies (e.g., policies that penalize honesty while permitting cheaters to "beat the system")
- Contradictory norms and community expectations
- A double standard (e.g., parents want the school to assure what they can't enforce themselves)
- A new age of majority (Reducing the age of adulthood to 18 has compounded attendance problems in many states.)
- Lack of court support in truancy cases (Traditional compulsory attendance has been rendered obsolete through court apathy in some areas.)
- Ineffective counseling services
- Limited extracurricular activities
- Lack of vocational education programs
- School phobia (To better understand this phenomenon, see the explanatory fact sheet that follows.)

SCHOOL PHOBIA

The following fact sheet is used in the White Bear Lake, MN, schools to help teachers better understand the nature of school phobia.

School Phobia **Truancy**
versus

School Phobia	Truancy
school often enjoyed; not delinquent or acting out; nor a behavior problem; responsive to internal problems; anxiety about being in school, somatic complaints; wants to get away from school and go home; intelligence adequate, often superior; overprotected, overindulged at home; parents not absent from home; parents aware of absences (may have made decision for them to stay home)	negative, inconsistent, antisocial: home, school, neighborhood, behavior problems, defiant; revolt against authority figures; not fearful about school; somatic complaints appear only if he or she is caught; often roams halls, doesn't go home; average or below average; lack of gratification at home; frequent disruption of family, which is often not aware that student is not in school

School avoidance
—poorly resolved parental dependency
—inadequate fulfillment of family relationships
—increase in dependency, regression
—parents are participants, often encouraging occurrences
—parents anxious about their own parents
—difficulty with expressions of anger; hostility dependent on parent
—child exploiting parents (bossy, manipulative, tyrannical)
—child may harbor hostility toward parents; sees angry feelings as a threat to parents' safety; fear of parental illness, death
—world is seen as a dangerous place (home is safe)
—reversal of parent-child roles, must stay home to care for parent

Family types that encourage school avoidance
—perfectionist, high expectations
—inadequate, multi-problem, welfare, chaos
—egocentric, focused on self, no support for others (often truants)
—unsocial, scapegoat for community, world not safe, paranoid

Family characteristics
—enmeshment, no separateness between members

—overprotectiveness, sense that the world is dangerous
—rigidity, same standards regardless of age
—lack of conflict resolution

School avoidance issues

Key issue is separation anxiety, which the child is ambivalent about. Avoidance of school is a symptom. These children are not malingering with somatic complaints. They do not fake symptoms; they actually make themselves sick. School refusal is much more serious as the child gets older—it may be evidence of a more serious disorder. Peaks are about 8 years and 11 or 12 (entry into junior high). Appears to be more frequent among only, first born, and last children. Most prone may be the "special child" (last chance kids, older parents, chronically ill, only boy, etc.). Of two types, (crisis, sudden onset or gradual onset), the crisis type has a better prognosis.

Regardless of cause, the toll taken on the school by excessive absenteeism far exceeds any simple violation of state laws or school rules. The adverse spinoff effects include: (a) lower achievement, (b) erosion of teacher and pupil morale, (c) increase in vandalism and crime, (d) loss of state financial aid, and (e) damaged public relations.

Unfortunately, many demographic indicators forecast that attendance problems will continue to grow throughout the 1980's. Most statistical studies point to more single-parent families, a growing number of minority and non-English speaking students, and greater numbers of pregnant young women of school age. All of these sociological factors are positively correlated with truancy and absenteeism.

To counteract these negative forces, the school must design an attainable master plan for maximizing regular attendance. The foundation for optimum attendance is a dynamic instructional program, but no matter how relevant and exciting the curriculum may be, it must be buttressed by an effective school attendance policy. The following are four sample policy statements that represent school-tested approaches to handling problems of truancy.

(Sample Policy #1)

POLICY ON TRUANCY

Ortonville (MN) Public Schools

A. First Offense

1. A conference will be set up with the student, assistant principal and/or counselor, and with the person reporting the violation.
2. A letter will be sent to the parent or guardian informing them of the student's offense and the action taken.
3. The parent or guardian must return to the school with the student, or otherwise meet acceptable readmission requirements.
4. The student must remain one-half hour after school for two weeks or double the time missed.
5. The student is to receive no credit for grading purposes for week missed during the period of truancy.
6. The work missed must be made up for credit.

B. Second Offense

1. A conference will be set up with the student, assistant principal and/or counselor and the person reporting the violation.
2. A letter will be sent to the parent or guardian informing them of the student's offense and the action taken.
3. A parent-student-assistant principal conference must be arranged by the parent or guardian to be held in the assistant principal's office no later than a designated date stated in the letter to the parent or guardian.
4. The student will be suspended from school for three days.
5. The student must remain one-half hour after school for three weeks.
6. The work missed must be made up for course credit.

7. The student will be sent home immediately if any of the above conditions are violated.

8. Future absences will be excused for illness only. The parent is to call in whenever the student is absent.

C. Third Offense

1. Third offense truancy will result in immediate dismissal without any specified provision for reentry. Students shall be given a copy of the Pupil Fair Dismissal Act. Students under the age of compulsory attendance law will be reported to the proper authorities for disposition.

(Sample Policy #2)

ATTENDANCE

Plymouth-Canton (MI) Community Schools

Students are to be in attendance in each class they are scheduled for every day. Any student who is absent eight times during a semester without a verifiable excuse will be withdrawn from the class and assigned a grade of "W." A student who falls below five classes during a semester will be assigned to a directed study area for a time equal to the meeting time of the class from which he or she is withdrawn. Any student who falls below four classes may be placed on a reduced schedule and sent home for the period of time he or she is not in class. Any student who falls below three classes will be withdrawn from school for the remainder of the semester. In addition, three unexcused tardies will be equated to one unexcused absence and counted toward the eight unexcused absences for being removed from a class.

1. Truancy is the absence from school or from one or more scheduled assignment without the authorization of the school. If the student is under the age of 16, truancy is a violation of the compulsory School Attendance Law....

2. Students who are under the age of 16 will be referred to the attendance officer for truancy and possible reassignment to class without credit.

(Sample Policy #3)

CLASS ATTENDANCE

Yorktown High School
Yorktown Heights, N.Y.

In order for a student to achieve success in his or her classes, regular and prompt attendance is vital. A cut is defined as an unexcused or unauthorized absence from a regularly scheduled assignment, including homeroom. Students who are having difficulty in a class or classes should see their counselor to discuss the problem. The school, at the same time, recognizes its responsibility to meet the needs of all students and, in particular, to provide appropriate alternative activities or programs for students whose extensive cutting has resulted in their removal from class.

The following procedures will be employed in response to the cutting of any class in Yorktown High School (including homeroom, study hall, and physical education):

1st Cut   One hour of after-school detention; phone call to parent; card sent home regarding the cut and explaining detention and penalties for future cutting, including the drop penalty outlined under "3rd cut."

2nd Cut   One hour of after-school detention; phone call to parent; card sent home as for Cut #1.

3rd Cut   One hour of after-school detention; card sent home; phone call to parent urging parent to contact the guidance counselor for a conference and informing the parent that the student will be dropped from class with "No Credit" or a "Drop F" and assigned to internal suspension for that period if he or she cuts that class for a fifth time.

4th Cut   Two hours of after-school detention; parents called and reminded of drop penalty; certified letter to parent; loss of student's free time by assignment to a study hall and requirement that student carry an attendance card for a period of time to be determined by the Grade Level Assistant for instruction/discipline.

5th Cut   Student is dropped from class with "No Credit." If the 5th cut occurs after the sixteenth week of the year, the grade recorded will be a "Drop F." Student is assigned to internal suspension for that class period pending an evaluation by school Pupil Personnel Services as part of a continuing effort to determine possible causes of such student behavior and to suggest alternative behaviors and/or possible alternative programs.

(Sample Policy #4)

STUDENT ATTENDANCE

Ligonier Valley (PA) School District

A. *Introduction*

1. Good attendance is essential for successful work in school. If the schools are to educate a student, he or she must not only be enrolled, but must also attend school regularly. Irregular school attendance should be recognized as a symptom resulting from factors in the school and/or home situation, or in the student's physical or emotional condition. Seldom does failure to attend school regularly result from any single factor but usually from a combination of factors.

2. College admissions offices and future employers use attendance records as a means of determining an applicant's dependability and good citizenship. To achieve your best in school, regular attendance is necessary.

3. Maximum educational achievement occurs for students through regular attendance in classes, while excessive absence results in the student's achievement below the level of expectancy and possibly even failure.

4. The intent of this policy is to provide a structure within which students can gain maximum benefit from the instructional program. Regular attendance in class is necessary if students are to receive

adequate guidance through their course work and benefit from the group dynamics generated within the class.

5. Attendance is and should be the responsibility of the parents and the students.

B. *Attendance Requirements*

1. The purpose of this policy is to place more of the responsibility for attendance on the student by making the earning of grades and credit directly contingent on his or her regular attendance. This is based on the premise that each class period contains instructional material or activities that are of significant importance to the student.

2. To be eligible to receive passing grades for a report card period, a student must attend at least 80 percent of the total number of scheduled student days for each report card period. In order to be eligible to receive passing grades for the complete school year, a student must attend at least 80 percent of the total number of scheduled student days for the year.

3. Students who are absent more than 20 percent of the scheduled class time for a grading period will receive a failing grade. Students who are absent 20 percent of a given year would be subject to the same penalty.

4. A student shall be deemed absent from a particular class whether the student failed to attend school at all on a particular day and therefore, was absent from all of his/her classes, or whether the student attended the school on a particular day, but cut or failed to attend a particular class.

5. Exceptions to these attendance standards may be made in special or unusual circumstances such as incapacitation due to illness or injury, hospitalization, or other administrative approved reasons for protracted absence.

6. In-school suspension will not be considered in calculating the 80 percent requirement for that grading period. However, out-of-school suspension will be considered as a student absence for purposes of calculating the 80 percent requirement....

7. The principal will be responsible for notifying the parents or guardians of any student who is in violation of the attendance requirements during any grading period in which failing grades are to be received and prior to the conclusion of the school year when a student's attendance record places him in jeopardy relative to being promoted or retained.

To enforce the school's policy on attendance (regardless of what form the policy takes), it is necessary to provide for routine and systematic recordkeeping and communication between the home and the school. For these purposes, the following representative forms may be helpful.

Grand Rapids Public Schools
Grand Rapids, Michigan

Date_____

Dear Parents/Guardian:

_____was marked absent from the class(es) on_____.

1st hour_____   5th hour_____
2nd hour_____   6th hour_____
3rd hour_____   7th hour_____
4th hour_____   8th hour_____

Our attendance office has not been contacted to excuse this student. Please call our attendance office as soon as possible.

Mora (MN) Public Schools

Mr./Mrs./Ms._____

Student:_____Grade_____
was shown being_____absent_____tardy

```
        Monday_____           Period 1____
        Tuesday_____                  2____
        Wednesday_____                   3____
        Thursday_____                  4____
        Friday_____                  5____
                                           6____
                                           7____

  He/she states:        _____Was there, was not absent
                        _____Tardy
                        _____No excuse
                        _____Other

  Detention assigned _____ Detention not assigned _____
  If this does not agree with your experience, see the principal.
```

Other workable ways to foster improved attendance, which should be considered, include the following:

- Establish a minimum number of days as a prerequisite for promotion.
- Study your school's "track record" and schedule important events and activities to attract and hold students in school when the absentee rate is usually the highest. (Many schools experience a weekly and yearly cycle where attendance is lowest on Mondays and during the month of May.)
- Release attendance figures by subject and class.
- Adjust the school calendar to accommodate popular family vacations/holiday periods.
- Establish Saturday makeup classes or require attendance at night school.
- Seek the cooperation of local physicians, dentists, etc., in scheduling student appointments during nonschool hours.
- Deny makeup rights for truants.
- Put attendance information in the hands of parents via regular newsletters, special mailings, etc., on a periodic basis. Publicize attendance problems when necessary to gain public attention and support.
- Use attendance as an indicator in teacher evaluation.

- Establish a wake-up service in special cases operated by parents and other volunteers.
- Encourage statewide school attendance review boards.
- Exempt student with perfect attendance from final tests.
- Use parents and other volunteers in the attendance office to make calls and home visits.
- If possible, reserve the right to determine the legality and legitimacy of all excuses.
- Provide incentives (e.g., certificates, T-shirts, pins) for perfect and near-perfect attendance.

As further guides to establishing successful anti-absenteeism programs, the real-life Attendance Action Plans described below provide models for reducing truancy in any school.

Attendance Action Plans

I. *Hudson (MI) Area Schools*—The Hudson Area Senior High School imposes a ten-day limit on absences during each semester. Any student who exceeds ten days must appear before the Attendance Board composed of one administrator, one counselor, and five teachers. The student must account for all absences. Action of the Attendance Board ranges from dropping the student from class to extending the absence period because of illness. Most frequently, students are placed on performance contracts.

II. *Penridge South Junior High School (Perkasie, PA)*—A weekly review is made of all absences by an Attendance Council (principal, assistant principal, counselor, nurse, and one teacher). Prompt action is taken where warranted with penalties ranging up to imposing a monetary fine on parents (permitted by Pennsylvania statute).

III. *Lawrence (KS) Public Schools*—An A.S.A.P. (Alternative to Suspension for Attendance Problems) program has been introduced to solve problems that cause unexcused absences. After a third unexcused absence, a student has the option of remaining in school if he or she agrees to attend a zero hour (7:30 a.m.) A.S.A.P. group for two weeks. Pupil service personnel supervise the group. The format of the A.S.A.P. group work follows the pattern below:

Day 1   Orientation. Students are given an overview and informed that if class work improves, they may be excused from the last three group meetings. Feedback forms for teachers are distributed. Students are requested to write personal educational goals.

Day 2   Feedback forms are collected. Students who return these forms promptly are excused from the last meeting. Discussion deals with the role of the school.

Day 3   Students work on homework. A staff member meets individually with each student to assess present classwork and special needs. Tutorial help may be available.

Day 4   The topics for discussion are social skills and social problem solving.

Day 5   A continuation of the social-skills exercise. Role playing may be used. A study period is provided.

Day 6   Feedback forms are distributed. Discussion focuses on career plans and educational opportunities.

Day 7   Feedback forms are collected and discussed individually. Students showing improvement complete evaluation forms and are excused from the remaining meetings.

Days 8, 9, and 10   Continued discussion and exercises with remaining group members.

IV. *Albuquerque (NM) Public Schools*—The Albuquerque schools have developed an effective Student Referral Model for dealing with educational, attendance and behavioral problems (see Figure 2-1).

All of the ideas and suggestions outlined in Figure 2-1 spotlight practical approaches to reducing both chronic and casual truancy. Good discipline must begin with good attendance. Since no school can teach students in absentia, it is essential that

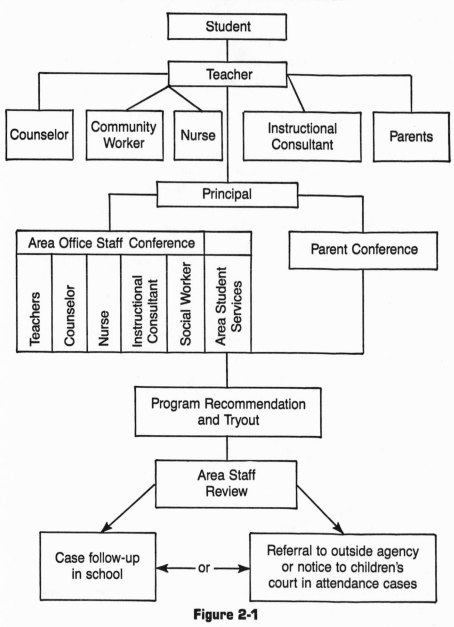

ALBUQUERQUE STUDENT REFERRAL MODEL

Figure 2-1

every staff member stress the importance of regular attendance every day.

Closely related to serious absenteeism are problems involving alcohol and drugs. When dealing with repeated truancy, school personnel often find that chemical abuse is a powerful contributing factor. The next section presents some extraordinary strategies for dealing with the persistent and expanding problem of drug abuse in today's schools.

WHAT TO DO ABOUT DRUGS

There can be no question that student drug abuse lies at the heart of many current behavior problems (e.g., truancy, vandalism, violence, etc.). As products of a drug-sodden society, today's youth (including elementary age students) are experimenting with a wide range of controlled substances to an extent unparalleled in this nation's history. Although the popularity of any specific drug may ebb and flow, overall drug usage by young people is expanding and moving down (fifth grade exposure is no longer uncommon in many areas). Since most educators are neither experts in pharmacology nor trained therapists, the school must recognize and accept its limitations in dealing with drug problems.

On the other hand, school authorities cannot ignore drug issues that may affect the health, safety, and education of all students. The primary concerns of school personnel regarding drugs and discipline fall into the following catagories:

- Student health
- Student achievement
- Attendance
- Order in the school
- Self-destructive and other destructive behavior
- Law violations
- Parent needs/concerns
- Peer pressure
- Consumption and sale
- Employee health/effectiveness
- Confidentiality
- Liability
- Legal limitations
- Student values (present and future)

As with most discipline dilemmas, no piecemeal approach is effective in dealing with the complex drug scene in most schools and communities. It is imperative, then, that school leaders become architects of a broad-based, master design for curbing and combating drug problems in schools. The essentials of such an organizational model for attacking drug-related discipline problems are explained below.

COMPONENTS OF A COMPREHENSIVE
CHEMICAL DEPENDENCY PROGRAM

I. Needs Assessment. To deal effectively with student drug use, the school staff must define and understand the dimensions of the problem in their particular situation. This requires calm, orderly information gathering, which focuses on the underlying issues.

Many schools find it helpful to conduct an anonymous drug usage student survey and to publicize the results as the basis for common understanding and coordinated action between the school and the community (see the sample survey form included below):

SAMPLE DRUG USAGE SURVEY INSTRUMENT

This Is a Confidential Survey
(circle your answers)

1. I have tried marijuana.		YES	NO
2. I usually smoke marijuana about once a week.		YES	NO
3. I often use marijuana three times a week or more.		YES	NO
4. I have tried alcohol.		YES	NO
5. I usually drink alcohol about once a week.		YES	NO
6. I often drink three times a week or more.		YES	NO
7. I have chosen to be abstinent (free from alcohol and other drugs).		YES	NO

II. Inservice Training. Any action taken by the staff pertaining to drugs in the school must be based on accurate information. The knowledge gap between students and staff regarding chemical use and abuse has often accentuated the problem and negated the school's efforts to improve the situation. Many students believe they know more than their teachers about drugs, and they are often right.

As a *minimum* this training should include complete coverage of the following areas:

- The facts of drug pharmacology
- Preventative measures
- Identification/recognition techniques
- Resources available (to staff, students, and parents)
- The concept of chemical dependency as a family disease

III. Drug Education. The only lasting way to diminish student drug problems (including alcohol abuse) is through a positive and powerful program of preventive education. Such a program should be introduced early (e.g., kindergarten and primary grades) and should be based on the realization that it is not the drug that is the problem, but the damage inflicted by the drug.

Well-intentioned program planners should also be cautioned that drug information alone (e.g., the facts of pharmacology) does not constitute a sound educational program. Most successful prevention curriculums stress *self-concept enhancement, esteem building,* and *self-respect development.* The goal is responsible decision making.

The essential learning outcomes of effective prevention education include the student competencies listed below:

- Recognizing and understanding the function of various drugs/mood modifiers
- Self-understanding (personal strengths/weaknesses)
- Understanding the biological and social determinants of behavior
- Knowing where to go for information/help and how to evaluate sources of information
- Understanding the legal issues involved in drug possession, sale, and consumption
- Developing understanding of a wide range of values about drugs
- Recognizing personal values concerning drug issues
- Developing techniques (coping skills) for handling stressful situations
- Self-accepting (a sense of personal autonomy)

IV. Policies and Procedures. Under today's circumstances, every school system (regardless of size) must have a set of systematized policies and procedures for both students and employees with problems of chemical abuse. Use of an Advisory Committee comprised of staff, parents, students, medical representatives, legal advisors, law enforcement representatives, and trained chemical dependency treatment specialists can be an invaluable resource in developing such policies and procedures.

The following flow chart provides a procedural "sequencing model," which some school authorities have found effective in handling student drug incidents.

In addition to incorporating the steps noted in the flow chart above, the school's procedures should be hard-hitting to be effective; but, at the same time, must reflect a strong emphatic understanding of the painful human issues involved in most chemical dependency problems.

The following suggestions should also be considered for inclusion in the district's drug procedures:

- Any action (e.g., penalty, intervention, referral) should be guided by what is best for the student.

- The need to prevent the actions of any individual from materially disturbing the good order and effective functioning of the school or from jeopardizing the welfare of other students must also be kept in mind.

- In handling students suspected of being under the influence of drugs, staff members should:

  a. remain calm and unhurried

  b. be thoughtful and discreet

  c. handle the situation with confidentiality

  d. quietly separate the student from the curiosity of onlookers

  e. handle the situation quickly and attract minimum attention

  f. refrain from accusing the student of drug abuses

- No staff member should retain any substance suspected to be nonprescribed drugs received from a student. Such substances should be returned to the student's parents or to the police for identification and disposition.

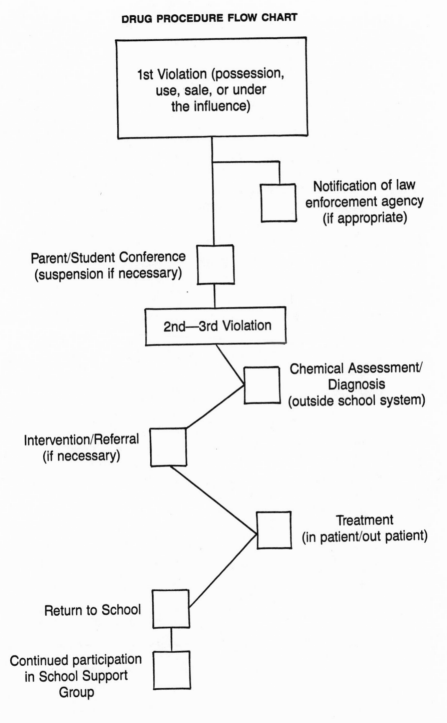

Figure 2-2

- Students who sell or attempt to sell substances suspected to be nonprescribed drugs should be referred to the police for appropriate action.

V. Specialized Personnel. More and more schools are finding it prudent to employ a cadre of professionally trained chemical dependency personnel. It is the size of the problem, rather than the size of the student body, that should determine the need for adding specialized chemical dependency staff members. The sample position description below illustrates the kinds of functions that can be performed effectively by such personnel.

(Sample Position Description)

CHEMICAL DEPENDENCY WORKER (K-12)

Responsibilities:

1. act as a resource to relevant existing programs and to staff members
2. assist with making referrals and with interventions for staff and students
3. be responsible for parent education and awareness programs at all levels
4. expand on the work presently being done with the Al-A-Teen, support, and growth groups actively participating when necessary
5. work directly with students and staff and serve as a resource to classroom activities
6. plan and provide continuing inservice training for appropriate staff on chemical dependency and mental health issues
7. be responsible for working with staff in developing and implementing preventive strategies, utilizing current effective education methods
8. be a liaison with community persons and agencies

VI. Legal Protectors. The statement below underscores that the school's chemical dependency program must be legally responsible:

It is clear that schools legally must respond when a student's health appears in jeopardy regarding drugs or alcohol; it is also clear that the school not assume the legal liabilities of a therapy center or hospital. Rather, the school must find a responsible and lawful interface with the state's health and human service system.

—*Bruce Bomier, Minnesota Behavior Institute, memo to school administrators, September 24, 1979*

In developing policy, initiating preventative programs, and taking disciplinary action related to drugs, school personnel should build in appropriate legal protectors, keeping the following three considerations in mind:

- Courts seldom overturn school board punishment of students for drug abuse.
- There is no double jeopardy involved in punishing students for school violations related to offenses for which there may also be legal penalties imposed.
- The school attorney should always be consulted if there is any doubt about the appropriateness or legality of any action.

VII. Support Groups. If the school honestly assumes responsibility for confronting the discipline and other problems related to student drug use, it is usually necessary to establish support groups for both users and "co-victims" within the school. These groups should be developed as needed at all levels (elementary and secondary) and should meet during school time. A trained leader is essential. The most common such groups involved in schools across the country include Al-A-Tots, Al-A-Teens, AA, etc.

VIII. Parent Education. No drug prevention program can succeed unless school personnel forge a bond of mutual concern and joint action with the parent community. The professional staff should use a variety of means to heighten parent awareness and understanding including newsletters, literature fairs, discussions, demonstrations, lectures, parent support groups, "hot lines," etc. It is imperative that parents be familiar with referral sources, available treatment centers, and family counseling programs in the community. Most comprehensive parent education programs on drugs focus on the following basic concerns shared by adults involved with youth and chemical abuse:

- Accurate drug information (avoiding overdramatization)
- Symptomatic behavioral/personality changes
- Communication strategies
- Preventative programs and measures
- The power of peer cultures
- Rehabilitation techniques and resources
- Parent pitfalls (e.g., sensationalism, scare tactics, moralizing, stereotyping)

IX. Employee Assistance. The district's anti-drug efforts are incomplete without some provision for recognizing and aiding chemically dependent adults in the school. The goal of an effective employee assistance program is treatment rather than censure. The "3 R's" of such a positive staff "wellness" program should be *reclamation, restoration,* and *renewal.* The sample personnel policy below exemplifies a common approach to employee assistance that has proved beneficial in many systems.

(Sample Policy)

CHEMICAL DEPENDENCY POLICY FOR EMPLOYEES

The School District recognizes chemical dependency as a treatable illness. District employees who are so diagnosed shall receive the same consideration and opportunity for treatment that is extended to employees with other types of illness. On the basis of medical certification, employees with the illness of chemical dependency shall qualify for the same health service benefits that are provided for other medically certified illnesses....

The District's concern with chemical dependency is limited to its effects on the employee's job performance. For purposes of this policy, chemical dependency is defined as an illness in which an employee's consumption of mood-altering chemicals repeatedly interferes with his or her job performance and/or adversely affects his or her health.

Supervisors will implement this policy in such a manner that no employee with chemical dependency will have his or her job security of promotional opportunity affected either by the diagnosis itself or by the employee's request for treatment.

If the employee refuses to accept diagnosis and treatment, or fails to respond to treatment, and the result of such refusal or failure is such that his or her job performance continues to be affected, it will be handled in the same way that similar refusal or treatment failure would be handled for any other illness. Implementation of this policy will not require or result in any special regulations, privileges, or exemptions from the standard administrative practice applicable to job performance requirements.

The confidential nature of the medical records of employees with chemical dependency will be preserved in the same manner as for all other medical records.

The purpose of this policy is to encourage recognition, early intervention, and subsequent support for the chemically dependent employee.

All of the elements outlined above are necessary features of an effective schoolwide effort to "get a handle" on drug-related discipline problems. In implementing this kind of divergent action plan, the cautions noted below must be kept in mind.

**TEN FATAL ERRORS IN FIGHTING
STUDENT DRUG PROBLEMS**

1. Underestimating the scope of the problem.
2. Relying on fear tactics.
3. Focusing solely on secondary students.
4. Stressing punitive approaches.
5. Treating alcohol differently than other drugs.
6. Minimizing parental involvement.
7. Assuming that all drugs are alike.
8. Adopting a puritanical (judgmental) perspective.
9. Presuming a chemically free staff.
10. Emulating a treatment center.

As one final rule of thumb, experience has shown that in emergency drug situations, it is usually best to *implement the least remedial measure and to seek professional help immediately.*

Although relatively minor compared to the trauma and pain associated with other drug problems, student smoking persists over time as one of the most frustrating and pernicious discipline issues confronting school staffs. The next "how to" section contains a variety of action steps for immediate use to help limit and eliminate student smoking problems.

TESTED TECHNIQUES
FOR CURBING AND CONTROLLING SMOKING

Recent statistics reflect a gradual reduction in the smoking population in this country. Unfortunately, student smoking does not seem to be decreasing at a proportionate rate and continues to be a major trouble spot in most secondary schools and some elementary schools as well. Even more disconcerting is that some studies show the number of girls smoking (particularly at the junior high level) is actually increasing. As with other drug usage, evidence indicates that most students who smoke begin because of peer pressure on the playground and elsewhere. If addiction is to occur, it most often seems to set in at about the tenth grade level.

Although the purchase, possession, and consumption of tobacco products by underage students is a flagrant violation of laws in almost every state, the school often emerges as the sole enforcer.

To a large extent, the courts, law enforcement agencies, and many parents have abdicated any responsibility for carrying out the letter of the law, while, at the same time, expecting and sometimes demanding that pupils not be permitted to smoke in school. Obviously, this is a no-win situation for school officials. Until society gets serious about prohibiting smoking by young people, the school cannot be completely successful in meeting such expectations. There are, however, a number of positive and productive steps that can be taken. Although there are no permanent panaceas, firsthand experience has proved that the measures below can go a long way in reducing student smoking violations:

- Identify designated smoking areas. A number of high schools throughout the country have experimented.with establishing formal student smoking lounges. Many of these efforts, however, have proved ill-fated and have been abandoned because of vandalism problems, legal questions, and difficulties in separating underage students from students who have reached the age of majority. Some schools have informally identified certain spaces, restrooms, etc., as "limited patrol" smoking areas for purposes of containing smoking in the building and providing some pollution-free areas for nonsmokers. The most practical approach seems to be to designate one or more *outside* areas for smoking and to engage student involvement in developing rules for use of the area.
- Give violators a choice between suspension and participation in a smoking seminar or a stop smoking clinic.
- Include accurate information on the effects of smoking in the regular instructional program and inform parents of where and when such units are taught in the curriculum and what materials and resources are available.
- Use interested high-school students to talk with junior high and elementary pupils about the risks of tobacco use.
- Impose limitations on faculty/staff smoking.
- Provide appropriate literature on health research and stop smoking programs in the school's library.
- Use group counseling and value clarification techniques to help students learn how to say *no*.
- Permit students to organize Nonsmokers Rights Groups.
- Display anti-smoking posters at strategic spots throughout the building.
- Celebrate local D-Days (stop smoking days).
- Elicit merchant support in the area to refrain from selling tobacco products to minors.
- Encourage students to conduct Cold Turkey Campaigns in the school.
- Display photographs of the unsightly aftermath and litter resulting from smoking in the school (e.g., entryways, foyers, restrooms).

- Confiscate cigarettes from underage pupils and send them to the parents with notification of a smoking violation.
- Use student contracts to help students control smoking at school or to eliminate the smoking habit entirely.
- Enforce a no smoking policy when adult groups use the building.
- Cooperate with the PTSA and other community groups to oppose local advertising aimed at youthful smokers.
- Adopt a firm and clear policy on student smoking. Now that using tobacco is less popular with many younger crowds, some schools are having increased success with "get tough" policies. (See sample policy below.)

(Sample Policy)

SMOKING BY STUDENTS

Montevideo (MN) Public Schools

Research and statistics demonstrate emphatically that smoking is injurious to one's health. However, the school neither condones nor condemns smoking or those who smoke. But, according to existing state laws and school policy, smoking is prohibited on school property and at school sponsored activities by any student. Students who insist upon smoking at school functions, or on school grounds (school, athletic fields, parking lots, etc.), will be identified and subject to the following disciplinary action:

1. A first-time violator may be assigned five hours of detention. The parents will be informed of the incident and the detention. The parents will also be informed of the suspension policy of the ... League that may affect school activities that their son or daughter may be in.

2. A second incident of smoking will result in suspension and the parents will be called and informed. A conference with the parents will be required for reinstatement.

3. Additional violations of the smoking policy will result in suspension from school for one day or less, and a conference with the parents will be required for

reinstatement. The objective is to get all people involved to discuss and agree upon an approach to solving the student's problem.

4. It is the student's responsibility to show up for detention. Failure to do so could result in suspension from school for one day. A conference with the parents will be arranged so that an approach to solving the student's problem can be agreed upon.

The law states that no one under 18 years of age can legally possess tobacco. Therefore, any student displaying or possessing tobacco will have such items confiscated and held in the office.

- Prosecute chronic offenders. With the accelerated passage of "clean air" statutes and ordinances in many areas, some school authorities are finding increasing support for imposing legal penalties on offending students. In Cudahy, Wisconsin, officials have noted a marked decrease in student smoking with the enactment of the ordinance below, which carries a $25 fine per incident and the potential loss of the student's driver's license if the fee remains unpaid.

**AN ORDINANCE TO PROHIBIT SMOKING
IN SCHOOLS OR PUBLIC LIBRARY**

5.13 (23) *No Smoking in Schools or Public Library.* It shall be unlawful to light a match or smoke, carry a lighted cigar, cigarette, or pipe in any school building or in the Cudahy Public Library except in areas approved for such purpose by the fire chief. It shall be the duty of the person or persons in charge of such building to post and maintain approved signs bearing the words *No Smoking* in locations designated by the fire chief or his representative.

Any educational or disciplinary action program, which the school may undertake regarding smoking, should be guided by the fact that fear is *not* a sufficient deterrent for most students. Repeated studies reveal that both users and nonusers are equally knowledgeable about the harmful health effects of smoking. A successful smoking reduction program, then, must feature a varied array of strategies such as those outlined above.

One frequent byproduct of drug usage (and to a lesser degree, smoking) is increased school theft. Students often steal to act out hostility while under the influence of chemicals and/or to support a costly habit. The next segment suggests school-tested helps to halt theft by students.

STEPS TO STOP STEALING

Some student stealing occurs in all schools. In fact, experimenting with theft seems to be a necessary part of the "growing-learning-testing" process for certain pupils. Nevertheless, frequent acts of stealing (from students, from staff, or from the school in general) undermine morale, destroy confidence, and threaten the entire climate of control in the school.

Although most student theft involves amounts of less than $10, certain areas in the school are particularly vulnerable to major losses and require special security attention. These include: the audio visual department, music rooms (especially where speakers and stereo equipment are stored), computer areas, and theaters.

The most common safeguards for providing adequate theft protection in schools are outlined in Figure 2-3.

Some research reports indicate that schools are about five times as likely to be burglarized as stores. In many cases, schools are victims of stealing because of some combination of the following faults:

a. serious drug problems

b. racial unrest

c. an excessive stress on competition (a clash of the "haves" and "have nots")

d. undue temptation (easy access to the property of others)

e. overly harsh demands of peer acceptance

f. an impersonal atmosphere in the school

g. an image of the school as a symbol/center for failure

STEPS TO STOP STEALING

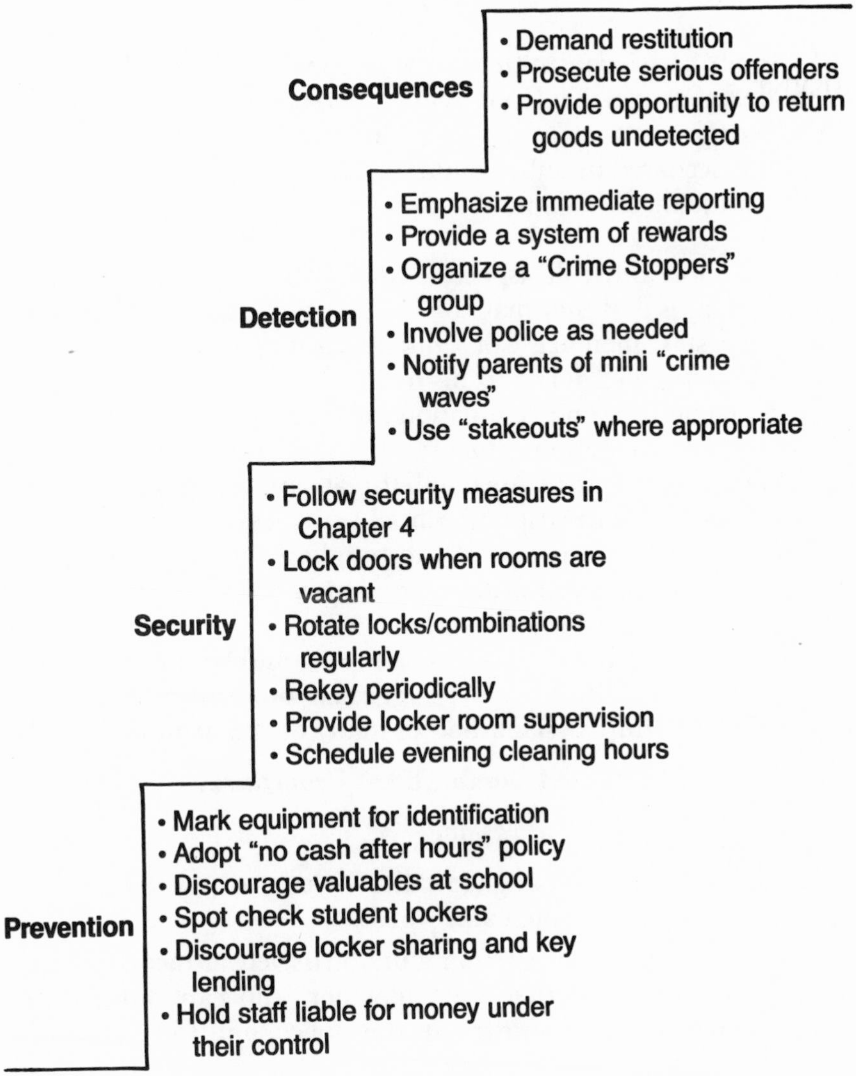

Consequences
- Demand restitution
- Prosecute serious offenders
- Provide opportunity to return goods undetected

Detection
- Emphasize immediate reporting
- Provide a system of rewards
- Organize a "Crime Stoppers" group
- Involve police as needed
- Notify parents of mini "crime waves"
- Use "stakeouts" where appropriate

Security
- Follow security measures in Chapter 4
- Lock doors when rooms are vacant
- Rotate locks/combinations regularly
- Rekey periodically
- Provide locker room supervision
- Schedule evening cleaning hours

Prevention
- Mark equipment for identification
- Adopt "no cash after hours" policy
- Discourage valuables at school
- Spot check student lockers
- Discourage locker sharing and key lending
- Hold staff liable for money under their control

Figure 2-3

When the school is plagued by a high incidence of theft, officials should look to these sources for lasting solutions.

The final chronic discipline bugaboo to be examined in this chapter is sometimes the most exasperating and potentially the most deadly. This section identifies workable ways for handling bombs and bomb threats in the school.

A REALISTIC RESPONSE TO BOMB THREATS

Bomb scares constitute one of the most ominous discipline situations that can confront school personnel. Although most threats are hoaxes and often come in cycles, enough real bombings have occurred in public buildings that every such threat must receive immediate, total, and serious attention by the officials in charge.

The most difficult aspect of anticipating and dealing with bomb threats is that they may come at any time and be received by almost any staff member. Consequently, it is critical that everyone on the staff fully understand his or her potential role if involved in an actual bomb scene. Simulation exercises can assist the staff in preparing for such an eventuality.

The central issue in any bomb threat situation is the question of whether or not to suspend school activities and evacuate the premises. This often is one of the toughest discipline decisions required of school authorities. *The responsibility for making this decision must rest with the building principal.*

The effective handling of bomb threats and bomb discoveries requires precise planning. The suggested procedures below are typical of procedures established in many of the nation's schools.

Suggested Bomb Threat Procedures

A. *In the event of threat or warning*

1. Receiver should engage caller as long as possible. Try to remember or note exact words.

2. If possible, receiver should unobtrusively attract the attention of some other staff member who can contact the appropriate administrator, the police, and the telephone company.

3. Receiver should attempt to determine:

   a. Location of bomb

   b. When bomb is set to explode

   c. Is bomb open or disguised

   d. Type/size of bomb

   e. Name of caller

   f. Estimated age/sex of caller

4. Principal or designee should inform district office and alert staff (some schools have developed a code for this purpose to avoid panic).

5. Evacuation decision by principal or designee:

   a. Decision must be based on the individual circumstances of the situation.

   b. Administrator should consult with police before making a final judgment.

   c. If evacuation occurs, students should be advised not to touch anything unusual during the process.

6. Conduct search of building with public safety personnel (staff members should be advised not to touch anything):

   a. Radio communications should be maintained throughout the search.

7. Principal or designee, should consult with police to determine when reentry will be permitted.

B. *In the event of actual bomb discovery*

   1. Staff should not touch or move any unidentified objects.

   2. Principal or designee should notify police and clear the area (fire drill procedures may be used for this purpose).

   3. Principal or designee should verify that the area is clear (teachers should take roll immediately after evacuation).

   4. School personnel should rely on the professional bomb squad to defuse or remove the bomb.

   5. Principal or designee should consult with police to determine when reentry will be permitted.

The Bomb Threat Checklist Form and sample policies on the next few pages provide further hints for managing real or threatened bomb situations.

BOMB THREAT CHECKLIST FORM

Grand Rapids (MI) Public Schools

Date _____ Time _____

Person Receiving Call _____

Phone number on which call was received _____

Building code _____

Information given by caller:

  Where is bomb placed? _____

  Why was it placed? _____

  When is it to go off? _____

  What does it look like?_____

  What type of explosive? _____

  Other information _____

Voice characteristics _____
  (loud, soft, raspy, high pitched, pleasant, deep)

Mannerisms _____
  (calm, angry, rational, irrational, coherent, incoherent, deliberate, emotional, laughing)

Speech _____
  (slow, fast, distinct, distorted, nasal, stutter, slurred, lisp)

Background noises _____
  (machines, trains, animals, music, quiet, bells, sirens, voices, office machines)

Caller's ID _____
  (male, female, adult, juvenile, approximate age—your opinion)

Language _____
  (excellent, good, fair, poor, foul, slang)

Accent _____
  (local, foreign, ethnic)

Other comments _____

This form is to be hand delivered or sent to the Public Safety office only. Copies may be made for administration and/or the police upon request.

(Sample Policy)

BOMB THREATS

Struther City (Ohio) Schools

In the event of a call or notice to the effect that a bomb has been placed in a Struther school building or establishment, the following procedures are recommended:

1. Immediate evacuation of the school or building.

2. If the call was not received originally by the fire and police departments, immediate notification is required. Both departments should respond.

3. A search of the building or premises should be conducted under the discretion of the senior officer present from either protective department. All officers, firefighters, and custodians of the building should assist in the search.

4. Circumstances will dictate whether any strange or foreign objects should be removed immediately or left for removal by a qualified person.

5. If a thorough search is conducted and nothing is found, the chief administrative officer of the school or building should be notified by the senior member of the local protective department that reentry will be permitted.

6. Investigation of the incident should be made by the local police department assisted by the State Fire Marshal's office, if requested.

Any decision concerning the dismissal of school pupils and subsequent action after the above procedures have been followed is the prerogative of the Superintendent.

(Sample Policy)

**DISCOVERY OF SUSPECTED BOMB
IN BUILDING OR ON GROUNDS**

Cedar Rapids (IA) Community Schools

A. Employee who discovers bomb or suspicious item—

    1. *Do not remove or handle bomb.*

    2. Clear area immediately.

    3. Notify Cedar Rapids Police Department.

B. Building Administrator (or designee)—

    1. Ensure that building is evacuated.

    2. Notify building custodian and nurse (health secretary).

    3. Notify buildings and grounds.

4. Activate plan to locate students at nearest facility if situation requires temporary student protection.

5. Contact Superintendent's Office if there is sufficient reason to consider cancellation of school.

As indicated earlier, no bomb situation can be taken lightly. Each instance requires firm, unequivocal decision making and action. In following up any bomb scare where violators are identified, school authorities should relentlessly prosecute the offender(s). It is also advisable to minimize publicity as much as possible to diminish the power of suggestion.

In conclusion, if teachers and administrators can establish effective mechanisms for dealing with the perennial bugaboos treated in this chapter, they are well on the way to assuring responsible discipline throughout the school. Chapter 3 discusses some definitive approaches to maintaining control of the most volatile and vulnerable spaces in the school.

3

How to Handle
Special Problem Areas
in the School

Many school discipline problems result simply from an unfortunate mix of time, space, and numbers. Every school facility contains certain special problem areas (e.g., hallways, restrooms, the cafeteria, parking lots), which lend themselves to troublesome mixes and generate a malproportion of disruptive or disturbing behavior that can spill over into the classroom. Careful attention to these areas, along with certain simple preventive measures, can often avoid or reduce potential problems. This chapter describes a variety of steps to help neutralize these persistent and perplexing trouble spots.

GUIDELINES FOR DEFUSING DIFFICULT SPACES

The following guidelines can help the school staff head off problems before they start:

1. *Identify and diagnose problem centers.* In order to prevent trouble, school personnel must know where it begins. An important first step is to chart and record each discipline incident for a period of a month or more with special attention to where it started. This kind of record enables the staff to analyze the focal points within the building or grounds that require special preventive or corrective actions.

2. *Minimize congestion.* Size is significant. Too many students in too small a space always breeds outbreaks of problem behavior. Just as a crowded classroom fosters short tempers, jostling, pestering, etc., congested hallways, foyers, restrooms, and lunchrooms inevitably lead to nuisance behavior that can escalate into minor upheaval at any time. Any steps that diminish or eliminate congestion within commonly used areas of the school plant will likewise reduce tension and incidents of inflammatory behavior. It is important that the school administrator keep traffic flow in mind while developing the school schedule, room assignments, activity plans, etc. Helpful tools in easing congestion may include staggering starting and dismissal times, and dispensing bus pickup points to various exits of the building so that the number of students congregated in a given area is minimal.

3. *Provide adult presence.* The single most effective deterrent to student horseplay and trouble making in school is the presence and visibility of adult staff members. This is as true in the hallways and the gymnasium as it is in the classroom. Unfortunately, recent provisions in many negotiated contracts and the addition of specialized security personnel to school staffs sometimes create a reluctance on the part of teachers to be outside of their classroom during passing periods and other busy nonclass times of the day. Where there are particular trouble-prone areas in a building, it is crucial that key adults on the staff be present to provide needed supervision during peak periods of use. The principal cannot be exempt from this responsibility and can provide a meaningful model for the entire staff.

4. *Prohibit certain articles.* As a preventive measure some schools find it helpful to prohibit students from bringing certain articles (e.g., slingshots, knives, toy guns) to school, which may provide undue and unneeded temptation and serve as a catalyst for a number of minor calamaties in hallways, restrooms, or other gathering places. Such steps are usually more effective at the elementary level. The Stillwater, Minnesota Public Schools have experienced some success in avoiding disruptive behavior by adopting the following regulations:

> *Problems arise each year because students bring articles that are hazards to the safety of others or interfere in some way with school procedure. Such items as lighters, water pistols, radios, and tape recorders, if brought to school as playthings, are*

undesirable and will be impounded and returned to the parent at his or her request. Parents are requested to help children understand the necessity for such regulations.

5. *Emphasize "respect" education.* Every school staff at all levels should continually stress the importance of mutual respect among students. An educational program or courtesy campaign within the school can help promote an atmosphere in busy or crowded problem areas that limits inappropriate actions by students. The following examples of *corridor courtesy* illustrate the kind of common-sense rules that need to be emphasized repeatedly to both elementary and secondary students:

- Always keep to the right in corridors and on stairways.
- Do not congregate in groups that block the flow of traffic.
- Refrain from running, pushing, excessive noise, and other types of discourteous conduct.

As part of an educational program designed to help students develop a social conscience based on respect for persons and property, the Stratham Memorial School in New Hampshire has included the following position statement in its discipline procedure manual:

Children should be constantly reminded of the rights of other people. This includes the rights of other students in various classrooms in the building to a quiet school environment and is reflected in the standards of behavior established for corridors, the library, restrooms, and other areas within the school building.

To maintain positive and productive norms of behavior in all parts of the school at all times, every teacher must be a teacher of respect.

6. *Vary the mix of students.* One of the best ways to short circuit explosive situations is to manipulate the mix of students who are clustered together at the same time in those areas of the school that are particularly troublesome. Many administrators find it advisable to avoid assigning all of the lockers of students in the same grade level in the same section of the building. Other options include varying seating assignments in assembly programs so that different grade levels are interspersed, and break-

ing up certain cliques and groups in the school by selective scheduling of lunch periods, etc. It pays for teachers and administrators to be students of the chemistry of their student body and to avoid creating undesirable combinations of individuals and groups wherever possible.

In addition to the general guidelines outlined above, the remainder of this chapter focuses on more specific strategies for limiting or alleviating undesirable discipline situations in trouble-prone areas of school.

KEY FACTORS IN KEEPING THE CAFETERIA CALM

Most administrators agree that the cafeteria/lunchroom is the most volatile area in the school. This is true at both the elementary and secondary levels. Lunchroom supervision is commonly viewed as the most distasteful and hazardous duty among the array of responsibilities that befall teachers. In some cities, the "mealtime madness" has become so tumultuous that schools have had to adjust their daily schedules in order to start and finish earlier and avoid serving any lunch to students.

There are, however, a number of practical steps that the staff can take to assure proper discipline and decorum in any school lunchroom. (See Sample Suggestions below.)

(Sample Suggestions)

TEN IDEAS FOR IMPROVING YOUR CAFETERIA

(Moundsview Public Schools, Moundsview, MN)

- Improve the place physically. Do wall murals. Launch a PTA project to buy some drapes or new furniture. Replace some gang tables with smaller ones.
- Organize a noon hour activity program. One school offers a different sports experience for pupils in the gym each week.
- Conduct an inservice program for the cafeteria supervisors. Arrange for the supervisors to meet periodically with a faculty sponsor and a group of pupils to discuss problems and solutions.

- Enlist the aid of student service groups to help keep the cafeteria clean.
- Modify the school's schedule so that long lines are made shorter and so that the total number of pupils in the room at one time is reduced to the lowest possible number.
- Form a menu planning committee.
- Start a breakfast program and encourage teachers to eat breakfast with students. There is evidence that many school breakfast programs reduce student absenteeism.
- Review the rules of conduct for students in the cafeteria. Eliminate the unenforceable ones and devise ways to enforce those remaining in an unobtrusive, routine manner.
- Start a "We're Proud of Our Cafeteria" publicity campaign with posters, school paper articles, class meetings, and assemblies.
- Provide a method of isolating chronic troublemakers.

The key element to maintaining order in the lunchroom is supervision. It is both foolhardy and unfair to assume that cooks can provide supervision while serving meals. In some cases, support staff such as lunchroom aides or monitors can play a primary role in maintaining order and discipline. In extreme instances, however, there is no substitute for the presence and influence of certified staff members (including the principal and assistant principal if necessary) in the cafeteria.

Some schools include lunchroom supervision as part of selected teachers' regular assignments (in lieu of one class assignment). This is an expensive form of supervision, but it may well be worth the cost to assure effective control. If the noon period is disrupted, the entire following afternoon of instruction may be jeopardized or impaired. Thus, adequate cafeteria supervision, regardless of cost, is often a wise investment in structuring the total day's environment for education.

The second most important factor in promoting positive behavior in the lunchroom is the lunch itself. The menu makes a difference! If the food served in the school lunch is not appetizing, interesting, and appealing, some trouble is inevitable. The spector of a legendary "food fight" haunts every school principal and cafeteria supervisor. The only sure-fire preventive measure is an attractive and varied menu *designed with children in mind.*

Despite the protests of "Type A lunch purists," alternative menu choices (e.g., salads or hamburgers) can go a long way in reducing cafeteria conflicts. In some cases, it is also helpful to vary the style of serving by introducing a family-style lunch occasionally. Where lunchroom unrest persists, the staff may be well advised to consider implementing an "open lunch" policy as a means of providing a necessary escape valve. One further effective means of promoting better behavior in the cafeteria is to involve students in food selection and menu planning.

Another positive step in keeping the cafeteria "cool" is to arrange for adults to eat with the students. Despite the allure, sanctity, and soothing effects of a separate faculty lunchroom, it is extremely helpful if at least some of the teachers can eat lunch with the students on a daily basis. Inviting parents, senior citizens, and other adults in the community to sample the school lunch periodically can also have a stabilizing effect on the cafeteria scene.

Whatever steps are taken to maintain an orderly lunchroom atmosphere, it is imperative that these efforts be undergirded by a clear-cut cafeteria policy about which both parents and students are thoroughly informed.

The following statement from the Loredo Elementary School (Aurora, Colorado) serves as a good example of such a positive policy.

Cafeteria Responsibilities

To help make our cafeteria a pleasant and safe place to eat, good cafeteria rules require that I—

- talk quietly and only to the people next to me.
- stay in my own place in line.
- handle only the silverware I'm going to use.
- be courteous to the aides and cooks who are trying to help me.
- make no unnecessary noises (popping bags, rattling tables, etc.).

- at least taste the food and definitely eat more than milk and dessert.
- remain seated while eating.
- not trade food with others.
- practice good home table manners.
- eat only in the cafeteria.
- raise my hand when I'm through eating and wait to be dismissed.
- bring my coat, boots, playground balls, etc., with me or do without.
- walk at all times.

If I find that I cannot follow these responsibilities, I realize that I will not be able to eat in the cafeteria anymore and will bring a sack lunch to eat someplace other than the cafeteria, or lose recess privileges because of my behavior. I may also be asked to write an explanation of my behavior, which may be sent home to Mom and Dad.

HOW TO MAINTAIN ORDER ON THE PLAYGROUND

The school playground constitutes the highest risk area for discipline problems at the elementary level. For this reason, the teachers and administrators must make special efforts to preserve orderly conduct in and around all play areas. The following suggestions can provide the framework for safe and successful playground management:

- Limit the numbers of students on the playground at any one time.
- Identify designated play areas for pupils of different size, age, and grade levels. Where practical, establish buffer zones between the assigned areas.
- Have a planned program of playground activities.
- Allocate the first five minutes of recess or playtime for a supervised group exercise program to "work off steam."
- Maximize supervision. Where possible, teachers should be visible on the playground during recess periods. Paid aides,

monitors, and volunteers can assist with supervision (see Playground Aide Qualifications). Older students can also be used occasionally to supervise the play of younger children.

Playground Aide Qualifications

1. Human relations/communications skills
2. Patience
3. Genuine liking of children
4. Enjoyment of the out of doors
5. Sound judgment (fair and impartial)
6. Ability to discipline large groups of children
7. Skill in handling first aid medical emergencies
8. Ability to be heard

- Maintain safe and functional playground equipment.
- Prohibit unduly dangerous activities (e.g., wrestling, tackle football, snowballing, etc.).
- Prohibit all vehicles, bicycles, motor bikes, etc., from the play area at all times.
- Involve students in developing reasonable playground rules. Ensure that students fully understand the rationale for all rules and regulations. All statements of rules should spell out the specific consequences of acts of inappropriate behavior (e.g., the Cedar Way Elementary School in Mountlake Terrace, Washington uses a simple written exercise for first offenders—see form below).

PLAYGROUND OFFENSE WRITTEN EXERCISE FORM

Student Name _____

Room _____ Date _____

The following sentences will be written five times each during loss of recess. If not completed, the number will be *double*.

School rules will be obeyed always.

Everyone deserves respect from others.
Courtesy and common sense pays.
Our playground needs my cooperation.
These rules are easy to follow.

- Consider substituting daily physical education periods for the traditional, free-play recess.
- Involve teachers and aides in playground games and activities.

A good example of a sound and effective overall playground policy, which brings together many of these suggestions, appears below.

(Sample Policy)

PLAYGROUND DISCIPLINE CODE

Lincoln Elementary School
White Bear Lake, MN

The playground is designed to be a place where children can play individually or in group activities during and after school hours. To provide for an atmosphere that is safe and fair to all students the following procedures and regulations have been developed. It will be the responsibility of all students to:

a. Demonstrate by their conduct and attitude that they respect the rights of others.

b. Use the playground apparatus and equipment in a safe and proper way.

c. Play out of doors when weather conditions are acceptable before school and during the noon hour unless they have written permission by parents or teachers to remain indoors.

d. Help keep the playground free of litter by placing litter in the proper receptacles.

e. Cooperate at all times with the school patrol.

f. Play away from the building so that classes in session will not be disturbed or building facilities damaged.

g. Line up by grade level when morning and afternoon bells ring.

h. Refrain from participating in rough play or games that invariably result in someone being hurt (e.g., tackle football, king of the hill, snowballing, handball, and rugby).

i. Cooperate at all times with the playground supervisor.

EFFECTIVE PARKING LOT CONTROL

In terms of potential risk, hazard, and nuisance problems, the parking lot is to the secondary school what the playground is to the elementary school. A recent survey of Minnesota high schools revealed the following problems associated with student parking lots:

1. Speeding
2. Reckless driving
3. Thefts from cars
4. Property damage/vandalism
5. Loitering
6. Littering
7. Noisy driving/disturbance
8. Gathering place for outsiders/intruders
9. Students arrive late and leave early
10. Students leave during the school day
11. Students use cars to smoke
12. Students use cars for romantic rendezvous'
13. Students use cars for consuming and exchanging alcohol or drugs
14. Students park in the neighborhood
15. Students violate restricted commercial parking

The obvious potential for disruptive behavior and discipline problems originating in student parking lots demands attention from the entire school community. Often the behavior, attitudes, and emotions generated in the parking lot carry over into the school and the classrooms themselves. In dealing with the myriad problems related to parking areas, the following measures have been most commonly imposed by schools throughout the country with varying degrees of success:

- Require registration of all motor vehicles and proper ID.
- Control access to student parking lots.
- Separate student, staff, and visitors' parking areas.
- Separate bicycle parking areas from automobile parking lots.
- Limit and/or discourage student driving to school (see Sample Parent Letter below).

(Sample Parent Letter)

St. Louis Park Senior High School
St. Louis Park, Minnesota

Dear Parent:

The newspapers carry articles about the increasing costs of fuel, the idea of a four-day work week, and the real possibility of gasoline rationing. Yet, our students have not moderated their driving to school.

I am asking you to have your students drive only when it is absolutely necessary, e.g., work, appointments, etc. The school bus should be used as the mode of transportation to and from school.

In addition to conserving energy, I consider the automobile to be an "attractive nuisance" for the teenager. The problems associated are late arrival to school, leaving early, using the cars to smoke, careless driving, vandalism to cars, and thefts from cars.

Many of these problems can be eliminated by changing the driving habits of our students. I ask for your cooperation and ask that you discuss my concerns with your son or daughter and seek his or her cooperation also.

Sincerely,

Richard L. Wainio
Principal

- Provide adequate supervision and surveillance (e.g., off-duty police, regular police patrols, school security personnel, other staff members, etc.). Some schools have reduced parking lot problems by utilizing Student Volunteer Patrols who have a vested interest in automobile/property protection. (If it's their car, it's different!)
- Provide ample lighting.
- Establish a student parking fee.
- Reduce speeds—install *speed bumps*. (In some climates, however, such installation compounds problems of snow removal.)
- Contract a towing service to deal with violations and offenders.

One comprehensive approach to exercising effective parking lot control is reflected in the model policy below:

(Model Policy)

PARKING AND TRAFFIC VIOLATIONS

A. All students, faculty, and staff who plan to use the parking facilities of the school must register each motor vehicle and secure a parking permit in the principal's office.

1. The car registration form to be completed shall include the license number, make of the car, model, year, name and address of the driver and his or her signature. It shall also indicate by schedule or location such information that will facilitate reaching the driver in the event that there is an emergency.

2. A parking permit (decal or sticker) shall be issued and attached to the lower left-hand corners of the rear-most window on the left-hand side and in no other place.

B. All students, faculty, and staff who are registered and display the permit must park in the lot designated.

C. Motor vehicles are not permitted to park in the following designated areas:

1. Fire lanes
2. No park zones

D. Motor vehicles are not permitted to occupy the following designated areas:

1. Any parking stall beyond the posted time limit.

2. Parking stall marked *Reserved*.

3. More than a single space marking a parking stall.

E. The speed limit in all parking lots shall be ten miles per hour.

F. Students are not permitted to occupy or operate a motor vehicle during the school day with the exception of those who are on cooperative work programs, special projects, or other assignments and have in their possession a permit granted by the assistant principal. Any other exception shall be by a pass issued with the approval of the school nurse and/or assistant principal.

G. Drivers of motor vehicles who violate the rules and regulations governing parking, traffic and safety shall be subject to the penalties that are applicable by the State and the City. Violations of the parking and traffic regulations of the school district will result in loss of permit, towing the vehicle at the owner's expense, or both.

H. For protection, parked vehicles should be locked at all times. The school district will not be responsible for any acts of vandalism, theft, and/or other losses or damages that occur.

WHAT TO DO ABOUT SCHOOL BUS BEHAVIOR

The familiar yellow school bus is an extension of the school itself. Thus, bus discipline must be a top priority concern for the school staff. Because of the safety hazards involved, this concern becomes even more critical than that for behavior problems in other special areas within the regular school building. "Bus woes" rank among the greatest headaches of school administrators throughout the nation.

In developing a safe and sound bus discipline program, the first issue that must be clarified is who has the ultimate responsibility for maintaining proper bus behavior (e.g., the contracted bus company, the district transportation director, the individual building administrators, etc.). Once this is established, a systematic procedure for ensuring bus control can be developed and carried out effectively.

The bulwark of a workable approach to positive bus behavior rests on a well-designed set of safety procedures and regulations and a sound program of safety education to disseminate these rules to all students, staff, and parents. Standard bus safety and behavior measures most commonly include the following:

- Students should line up a reasonable distance (ten feet) from the place designated as the bus stop. Single lines should be formed.
- Students should move a reasonable distance from the bus upon alighting before the bus leaves.
- Students should cross streets only after the bus is one-half block away from the bus stop.
- Students should respect the property rights of those people who own homes adjacent to bus stops.
- Once a bus is in motion, it will not stop for latecomers.
- Students should conduct themselves in a manner that will be helpful to the driver in observing traffic safety. Shouting, whistling, yelling, loud singing, and boisterous conduct that may distract the driver will not be tolerated.
- Students must follow the driver's instructions relative to seating arrangements.
- Students are never to stand when seating is available.
- Students shall ride only on the bus designated by the school principal.
- Students shall identify themselves upon request.
- The following acts will not be tolerated:

  a. snowballing in vicinity of bus stop

  b. hitching rides on rear of bus

  c. scuffling or pushing in line while waiting

  d. extending hands and arms from bus windows

  e. throwing items out of bus windows

  f. using improper language—making derogatory remarks

  g. any other act endangering health or safety

A second critical element in operating a well-disciplined school transportation program is a cadre of carefully selected, competent, fully trained drivers. Like teachers, school bus drivers must possess an unusual capacity for remaining calm under pressure. It sometimes takes courage to face one's problems, but it takes considerably greater heroics to continually handle problems with one's back to them. For this reason, the recruitment and selection of drivers is one of the most important personnel functions performed by or for the school district. Once selected, training in safety procedures and student discipline techniques should be updated for all drivers on a periodic basis. This training should emphasize that the most effective defense against discipline problems for school bus drivers is to *know the riders.*

In order to assure consistent enforcement of the bus discipline program, it is also essential to maintain a structured system for processing and recording infractions. The sample forms included below have assisted three school districts in operating this kind of system.

(Sample Form)

BUS INCIDENT REPORTS

Prior Lake Public Schools
Prior Lake, MN

Date _____ Bus Operator_____

Student's Name _____ Grade _____

Bus Operator's Statement of Incident _____

_____

_____

_____

Has there been previous contact with the parent?

_____ Yes   _____ No

Has the parent been contacted this time?

_____ Yes   _____ No

Has the child been denied transportation services by the driver and with the concurrence of the principal?

_____ Yes   _____ No

Number of days service denied _____

Commencing _____

(Sample Form)

VIOLATION OF SCHOOL BUS REGULATIONS

St. Louis Park Schools
St. Louis Park, MN

Student's Name _____ Date _____

Dear Parents:

Your (son/daughter) has had the violations checked below on Bus #_____.

1. Trespassing on lawn near bus stop
2. Failure to line up properly at bus stop
3. Standing too close to door before bus doors are opened
4. Arriving late at bus stop
5. Attempting to board bus after bus is in motion
6. Crossing street before bus is one-half block away
7. Failure to follow driver's instruction on seating
8. Boisterous or discourteous behavior
9. Eating or drinking on bus
10. Using improper or vulgar language
11. Riding wrong bus
12. Other_____

We have been charged with the responsibility for operating the buses according to rules established by the school administration. We urge parents and students to cooperate with us in our effort to furnish transportation that is both safe and efficient.

If you have any questions regarding the violation, call____.

Thank you for your cooperation.

Bus driver #_____

(Sample Form)

BUS REFERRAL REPORT

Grand Rapids Public Schools
Grand Rapids, Michigan

(Driver to Principal)

Date _____

Time _____   Bus #_____

Student name _____

School _____ Principal _____

On the above date and time the above student endangered the safety of all students riding the bus because his/her action diverted the driver's attention.

Explanation of Incident

_____

_____

This is to bring this matter to your attention and to request that you speak with the student and take whatever action you feel necessary to inform the student of his/her responsibilities for overall safety on the bus.

_____

Driver

(Sample Form)

PUPIL TRANSPORTATION STATUS REPORT

Grand Rapids Public Schools
Grand Rapids, Michigan

(Principal to Driver)

Date _____

School _____ Principal _____

Student _____

On the above date I spoke with _____
regarding his/her conduct on the bus.

I am herewith taking the following action:

☐ Spoke with student—readmission to the bus with full transportation service

☐ Removal of transportation service for the period

_____ days until _____

_____ weeks until _____

_____ remainder of school year

☐ Student informed

☐ Parent informed

_____
                                Principal

Comments:

_____

_____

In addition to the routine discipline procedures and precautions outlined above, it is important for the school transportation staff to have a specific action plan for emergency situations. The following extreme discipline procedure for bus drivers adopted by the Struthers City Schools (Struthers, Ohio) exemplifies such a plan:

a. Stop bus immediately at edge of road.

b. Turn off ignition.

c. Set emergency brake.

d. Separate the fighters (if applicable).

e. Notify the proper school official.

f. The school authority should have the parents involved come to the scene.

g. As a last resort, call the police to the scene.

In extreme circumstances and/or as preventive measures during high risk periods (e.g., initial stages of desegregation busing, preholiday periods, the last day of school, etc.), the following steps may also help avoid tense discipline situations:

- use extra staff members (drivers, teachers, administrators, aides, etc.,) to ride "shot gun" on all vulnerable buses.
- direct buses to follow alternate routes or slightly adjusted time schedules.

Further suggestions for encouraging and enforcing positive school bus behavior are contained in the sample policy included below.

(Sample Policy)

SCHOOL BUS POLICIES

Frazee-Vergas Public Schools
Frazee, Minnesota

Bus patrol—

It is recommended that the bus driver organize a bus patrol of at least two students. The duties of the school bus patrol will be to assist the driver in making reports, carrying messages, maintaining control of students on the bus, and such other duties as the driver may direct.

Handling of violations—

1. First violation ... the principal will hold a conference with the student and others as he (or she) deems necessary.

2. Second violation ... the student shall not be permitted to ride the bus until the parent or guardian, together with the student, has had a personal interview about the matter with the bus driver and the principal.

3. Third violation ... will result in automatic suspension until the case is heard by a final review board consisting of parents, students, and bus drivers, the principal and the superintendent. The review board shall have the power of suspension for a period not to exceed nine weeks and its decision shall be final.

In addition to restrictions, regulations, and enforcement procedures, an effective bus behavior program should include some incentive measures. An example of such a positive approach is the simple bus safety program for severe emotionally disturbed students in the Lorain (Ohio) City Schools outlined below.

Jane Lindsay "06" Program
(Lorain, Ohio)

BUS SAFETY RULES

1. Sit in assigned seat.
2. Use polite language—no swearing, no name calling.
3. Keep your hands to yourself—no hitting or throwing.
4. Obey the bus driver.

When you follow these safety rules you will earn:

—One bus pass for following these rules on the way to school.

—One bus pass for following these rules on the way home.

When a class brings in 100 bus passes without losing any, they will earn:

—One pizza for the class or sodas for the class.

When a person doesn't bring in a pass, the class must begin at zero.

STRATEGIES FOR CROWD CONTROL—
SUGGESTIONS FOR SAFE AND SANE
ATHLETIC CONTESTS

Of all of the special problem areas in the school, the gymnasium and athletic playing field pose the most unusual set of circumstances. The size of the crowds involved, which include large numbers of people from outside the regular student population; the emotionally charged atmosphere that is not only accepted, but actively encouraged; and the limelight of attention that is focused on athletic contests make student discipline and crowd control at sporting events a paramount concern for the total school staff. The reputation of the school and the general atmosphere of the student body is, perhaps, more on the line in these areas than in any other segment of the school.

The suggestions contained in this section have been tested and found effective in a variety of schools and school systems. A sound beginning for ensuring order at athletic contests lies in a comprehensive program of "fan education" for both students and adults. Some schools achieve positive results by conducting mini-clinics prior to each sports season. The purpose of these clinics is to review rules and to communicate the proper roles of players, coaches, officials, and spectators. Such clinics can play an important part in reasserting the supporting spirit of boosterism and in encouraging fans to assist school personnel in conducting safe and sane competition. Another effective technique for educating or reeducating fans regarding proper crowd behavior is to distribute bulletins or information sheets before each contest. An example of this type of handout is represented by the Guidelines for Good Spectator Sportsmanship included in this section.

**GUIDELINES FOR GOOD
SPECTATOR SPORTSMANSHIP**

(These guidelines are based on the
Minnesota State High School League's
Sportsmanship Project)

Essentially we ask you, the viewing public, to adhere to the following fundamental standards of good crowd conduct:

1. Maintain self-control at all times. Good sportsmanship is concerned with the behavior of all involved in the game.

2. Show respect for the opponent at all times. Good sportsmanship is the Golden Rule in action.

3. Show respect for the officials. Good sportsmanship implies the willingness to accept and abide by the decisions of the officials.

4. Know, understand, and appreciate the rules of the contest. A familiarity with the current rules of the game and their necessity to a fair contest is essential. Good sportsmanship is conforming to the spirit as well as to the letter of the rules.

5. Recognize and appreciate skill in performance regardless of affiliation. The ability to recognize quality in performance and the willingness to acknowledge it without regard to team membership is one of the most commendable gestures of good sportsmanship.

6. Show a positive attitude in cheering, refraining from intimidating or negative type of cheering. Good sportsmanship is cheering your own team on to victory.

Certain undesirable acts or actions by you, the viewing public, can't be condoned. Anyone found in violation of the following may be asked to leave the contest:

1. Use of obscene or abusive language that seeks to offend or intimidate a player, official, or spectator.

2. Use of noisemakers—examples: whistles, compressed airhorns, cowbell, etc.

3. Use of banners or placards.

4. Throwing of objects—examples: coins, pop cans, papers, etc.

5. Being on the premises of the scheduled contest while under the influence of alcohol or chemicals.

6. Unauthorized entry into any scheduled contest.

Keep in mind that as a spectator you are a guest of the school. Your token payment to an interscholastic contest entitles you to one thing—the privilege of watching students, amateur athletes, exhibit what they have learned in the athletic classroom. Think of the playing field as an extension of the classroom. Interscholastic athletics are justified only in this contest. *We're happy to have you here. Come again and enjoy amateur athletics at their finest.*

In setting the tone or standard for student behavior at athletic events, the coach is obviously a central actor. Every effort must be made to employ a quality coaching staff with both athletic and human relations skills and to conduct a meaningful performance review of all coaches on a routine basis. The kinds of expectations for coaches that are necessary to conduct an orderly athletic program are clearly outlined in the following excerpts from the Cedar Rapids, Iowa Athletic Handbook:

Sportsmanship of School Personnel

All personnel affiliated with a school involved in a contest are responsible to conduct themselves in such a manner as to represent the high ideals and principles of their school. The same is expected of the athletes, to demonstrate only the finest in sportsmanship. The adherence to good sportsmanship and good conduct by all personnel is the responsibility of each school member. There have been coaches who have removed a team from the field or floor and failed to finish the contest because of dissatisfaction with the officiating. This is a serious violation and the Board of Control will not tolerate such action. The coach has the responsibility of having the team appear for the contest and then return the team to its home school. Any coach who cannot assume these responsibilities should not have the privilege and honor of coaching in interscholastic athletics.

Ideals, Principles, and Standards for Coach's Conduct

If a coach's habits or conduct, either *in* or *out* of school, is such as to make the coach unworthy to represent the ideals, principles, and standards of interscholastic athletics, it is the duty of the school administrator to relieve the coach of all coaching responsibilities.

"No Cut" Philosophy

All coaches are to be aware of and comply with Cedar Rapids' unique "no cut" sports philosophy. Every eligible student is entitled to the privilege of trying out for a team, of becoming a member of the team, and of remaining on the team until the completion of the schedule for that sport.

Code of Ethics for Coaches to Be Used as a Guide for Professional Conduct

A coach should

- Be loyal to superiors and peers and support school policy.
- Have lofty ideals and fine principles of right and truth.
- Always strive for more education and culture.
- Be a goodwill ambassador between the school and the public.
- Teach and practice good sportsmanship.
- Be humble in victory and courageous in defeat.
- Neither knowingly nor unethically strive for another coach's job.
- Respect and support officials at all times.
- Never publicly criticize other coaches or officials.
- Offer congratulations in public—win or lose.
- Never "run up" the score.
- Dress in a manner suitable to the profession.
- Set an example of proper conduct that will earn the respect and confidence of all.

Relationship Between Coach and Players

The coach should always be aware of the tremendous influence the position wields, for good or bad. Parents entrust their dearest possessions to the coach's charge and the coach must always be sure that the young people are finer and more decent people for having been in athletics.

The coach should never place the value of a win above that of instilling the highest desirable ideals and character traits in players.

The safety and welfare of players should always be uppermost in the coach's mind and they must never be sacrificed for any personal prestige or selfish glory.

Coaches must remember that they are living examples for all of the young people in the community in which they coach. It is vitally important to the coach and to the profession that actions and behavior at all times bring credit to athletics.

The Coach's Leadership Role

The function of the coach is to educate students through participation in sports. This primary and basic function must never be disregarded. In teaching a sport the coach must realize that there are certain rules designed to protect the player and provide common standards for determining a winner and loser. Any attempts to beat these rules, to take unfair advantage of an opponent, or to teach deliberate unsportsmanlike conduct have no place in athletics.

The coach should set the example for winning without boasting and for losing without bitterness. A coach whose conduct reflects these principles need have no fear of failure, for in the final analysis the success of a coach can be measured in terms of the respect earned from players and from opponents.

The Coach and the School

Coaches must remember that they are on public display as representatives of public institutions. It is important, therefore, that their conduct be such as to maintain the principles, the integrity, and the dignity of the school.

School policy regarding athletics should be adhered to both in letter and in spirit. Coaches should remember that other members of the faculty also have an interest in the institution and its students and their conduct must be such that there arises no criticism of their efforts to develop the common interest and purposes of the school.

The Coach and Professional Contacts

It should be assumed that all members of the coaching profession are people of integrity and are making an honest effort to follow the precepts of this code. Therefore, opposing coaches should be treated courteously and as guests of the school. Moreover, the winning coach should make every effort to assure that the losing team be allowed to lose with dignity and leave the contest with its self-respect intact.

Sportswriters and sportscasters should not be used as means of relieving ill-feelings toward other coaches, players, officials, or other schools. They also have an interest in athletics and should be treated with the same respect and honesty that is expected of them.

Officials are an integral part of the game and it should be recognized that they also maintain high standards of integrity and honesty. Just as coaches can make mistakes, so can officials. It is important that their efforts to contribute to the education of young men and women through sports be recognized and supported.

One of the most aggressive steps that can be taken by school personnel to forestall trouble and foster a positive atmosphere at athletic contests is to launch a vigorous, full-blown sportsmanship campaign at both the school and the league level. Some schools utilize a fan-of-the-month contest to focus attention on positive crowd behavior. Another approach is to initiate a program of school sportsmanship awards. In an effort to improve the quality of fan performance at its highly emotional annual basketball tournament, the Minnesota State High School League has introduced a sportsmanship program including the following components:

- Three sportsmanship awards (one each day) are presented during both the girls and boys basketball tournaments.

- Sportsmanship activities (e.g., card section routines) are encouraged during all games, although signs and banners may not be involved.

- Halftime programs are made available to the schools to feature their cheering sections, bands, cheerleaders, drill teams, singing groups, dancelines, or other activities appropriate to the tournament.

- On the first two days of the tournament, one of the schools involved receives the daily award based on its activities before, during, and after the game, including the halftime presentation.

- On the final day of the tournament, the State Sportsmanship Trophy is presented to the school in each class that best characterizes and exhibits the highest qualities of good sportsmanship through the duration of the entire tournament.

Every special sportsmanship project should be accompanied by strong efforts to encourage and/or influence the media to report outstanding cases of good sportsmanship, as well as poor sportsmanship.

Another technique for using positive fan power to control contests is to "stack the stands." Security personnel, off-duty police officers, aides, and other school staff members can be interspersed throughout the crowd in order to be in an advantageous position to quell any disquieting behavior in its embryonic state. This should be accompanied by an all-out effort to encourage attendance by positive fans (e.g., parents, senior citizens, local dignitaries) through promotional gimmicks, special nights, and complimentary passes, where appropriate.

In spite of all of the positive efforts that the school may undertake to promote sportsmanlike conduct, there may be situations in which intense rivalries or other emotional overtones create potentially dangerous circumstances. Under these conditions, school officials may find it necessary to employ one or more of the following emergency procedures:

- Overloading security and surveillance in controlling access to playing and spectator areas.
- Varying the time of the contest (e.g., late afternoon, midweek).
- Limiting attendance to students and family. Some schools have found it necessary to ban junior high students from attending senior high games.
- If necessary, stopping the contest and removing any offenders.
- The Topeka, (KS) Public Schools have also found the following measures to be effective deterrents to disruption at particularly volatile contests:
  a. Video tape machines are provided for the purpose of video taping the audience should individuals within

the crowd feel impelled to disrupt the game. Video tape provides instant recognition of offenders.

b. The principal in charge meets prior to the game with the officials to convey unqualified support should it become necessary to suspend the game or clear the stands because of an unruly crowd.

c. Coaches at both schools involved address their respective student bodies prior to the game to stress the need for good sportsmanship before, during, and after the game.

d. Students in the competing schools who may have a potential for causing problems are counseled prior to the game.

e. Band directors at both schools are advised that while the ball is in play no performance should be given by the band.

• As a last resort in a crisis situation, the school staff should not hesitate to postpone, cancel, or forfeit any contest.

In most instances, the emergency steps outlined above will never have to be adopted. The school's athletic program can be one of the most vital instruments for promoting good discipline in all areas of school life. Usually, a few simple preventive strategies permit sporting contests to take place in a controlled manner and to exercise their powerful influence in generating pride and spirit among the student body.

This chapter has presented a number of easy-to-follow methods for preserving good discipline in and on the school's cafeteria playground, parking lot, buses, gymnasium, and playing fields. If positive attitudes and harmonious interpersonal/student-staff relationships are maintained in these special areas of the school, the staff will have gone a long way in winning the battle for better behavior throughout the entire school.

The next chapter treats the most extreme and worrisome discipline disturbances in the school setting—acts of vandalism and violence.

4

Tested Ways
to Deal with
Vandalism and Violence

Violence and vandalism, once low-incident disciplinary concerns, have now escalated to nationwide problems of major proportions. The conservative estimated cost of disruptive behavior in the public schools alone now far exceeds an annual amount of $12 million. More importantly, these disruptive manifestations of misbehavior impose an incalculable personal cost on thousands of students who are deprived of meaningful learning experiences because of a pervading atmosphere of suspicion and mistrust in the school.

This chapter offers unique and useful insights into the why and how of disruptive school behavior and a comprehensive collection of tested tips for handling vandalism and violence problems in your school.

Social scientists report that the cause of increased violence and vandalism in American schools are many and varied, including:

- growing urbanization
- deteriorating core cities
- poverty
- schools that are too large
- youth unemployment
- racial unrest

- family life and value changes
- television
- the growing presence of the "school intruder"
- erratic attendance and increased truancy
- politicalization of the schools
- a protracted period of adolescence, which has become a "bridge too long" for many young people

This information is of little consolation, however, to the students and parents who are frightened, staff members who are increasingly harassed, and taxpayers shocked by the nonproductive costs created by school damage and disruption.

If the business of education is to unfold in an orderly and effective fashion, the school must be more than extension of the street or the ghetto. It must be a special place where special things happen to everybody's children. This requires a minimum of disruptive behavior.

Repeated acts of vandalism and violence produce a psychological cycle that demeans learning and learners. Frustration and fear inevitably lead to some forms of acting out behavior (e.g., abuse of property or people). In turn, incidents (in some cases, epidemics) of vandalism and violence breed inreased fear and hostility in students. The tasks of education can be accomplished only if teachers and administrators intervene to abort this repeating pattern. The following sections provide practical suggestions for breaking the vicious cycle of vandalism and violence.

SUCCESSFUL STEPS TO PROMOTE PRIDE POWER AND IMPROVE BEHAVIOR

Any effort that boosts student pride in the school decreases the likelihood that acts of vandalism or violence will occur. Despite the acceleration of maturation in America, today's students are not too sophisticated to develop a strong feeling of pride and protectiveness for their school. A sense of belonging and a fierce feeling of loyalty to an in-group are crucial to all children and youth. These feelings can as readily be built around and focused on the school as on a gang, a club, or any other youth group. Once established, the peer pressure generated by genuine school pride is a powerful force in deterring disruptive acts. *Pride Power* can become the school staff's most effective preventive measure against vandalism and violence.

In addition to the traditional means of stimulating school spirit (e.g., pep rallies, bon fires, school songs, school banners, social events, etc.), the following approaches provide effective ways of promoting school pride and improving behavior.

Spirit Week

Many schools have experienced success in scheduling a spirit week sometime during the year, featuring a variety of daily activities (dress up day, hat day, etc.), designed to kindle camaraderie and spark school spirit.

Evening Ski Trips

One way of bolstering school pride and togetherness during the winter doldrums is to organize optional after-school ski trips for interested students and staff members. The costs of these excursions can often be defrayed through PTSA support or the allocation of miscellaneous activity funds. These fun moments of winter often become the fond memories of spring and help to establish positive relationships among the school family.

Flaunting School Colors and Symbols

Wearing and using school insignias, colors, and symbols are tangible expressions of school identity that reflect pride. Although promotions and sales to and/or by students in school are often discouraged to avoid undue exploitation, there are situations where legitimate student organizations need fund-raising opportunities. The sale of school T-shirts, caps, pins, sweatshirts, scarves, stationery, etc., provide one means of supporting worthy student activities while contributing to positive expressions of school identity and unity.

Positive Recognition of Achievement

A variety of efforts can be employed to honor and recognize student and staff accomplishments. Prominent displays of student work, featuring *students of the week* on bulletin boards and in school publications, awarding certificates of achievement at local school board meetings with appropriate press coverage, are all effective ways to foster peer pride and school spirit.

Fitness Programs for Students and Staff

Exercise classes and after-school joint jogging programs for both students and teachers at all levels can promote physical and socio-emotional health within the school.

Student/Staff Retreats

Many schools utilize some form of student/staff retreat to promote harmony and mutual respect coupled with an informal living-learning laboratory experience. Each year Sandburg Middle School in Anoka, Minnesota provides a two and one-half day environmental education retreat for all seventh graders and an appropriate number of supervising staff members in a rustic camp setting in northern Minnesota. As a result, both students and staff learn a great deal about science and ecology and, more importantly, about each other.

"Madison Avenue" Campaign for Your School

One effective means of engendering school pride is to involve the students in conducting a campaign to "sell" the school to others in the community. The six hints for advertising your school, listed below, can go a long way in making students proud of their school:

1. *Take productions on the road:* When school plays and other productions are performed in other schools and before adult groups outside the school (including nursing homes) the students involved receive extra learning experiences and the school enhances its image. Feedback from such road trips can do a great deal to boost school ego and reinforce school pride.

2. Involve students in developing a *film strip/video tape presentation* depicting outstanding features of the school. These presentations often serve as welcome programs for civic groups, local TV stations, PTA meetings, etc.

3. *Use available local marquees and billboards* (banks, restaurants, churches, etc.), to advertise and promote school events and activities.

4. Use a school FM radio station or local CATV channel to feature *success stories* from your school.

5. Spread the word—*Balloon Drift:* Release helium filled balloons containing fact sheets about the school and a coupon to return to the school indicating where the balloon landed. A prize can be offered for the coupon received from the farthest location from the school.

6. Develop *highlight* sheets emphasizing positive features of the school for distribution to prospective students, real estate brokers, and community groups (see following sample).

(Sample School Highlights Sheet)

HIGHLIGHTS

of

St. Louis Park Elementary Schools

(Off to a Good Start)

- Goal-based curriculum
- Team reading
- Multi-age grouping
- Forms of departmentalization
- Mini-courses
- Learning centers
- Cross-age tutoring
- Contract learning
- Independent study
- Parent-volunteer programs
- Flexibility and choice of reporting pupil progress
- Development in basic skills areas stressed
- Emphasis on affective learning
- Full-time physical education, vocal music instructors, librarian/media specialists
- Fifth and sixth grade band and orchestra
- Two elementary art specialists
- Comprehensive pupil services program—counseling, social work, health, speech therapy, diagnostic and psychological testing

- Special education classes—SLBP and EMR
- Summer school
- Full-time coordinator of programs for gifted and talented K-12
- Early kindergarten entrance for children who qualify
- Student teaching center
- Preschool/daycare program
- Title I—reading and math

History of the School

Involving students in compiling and publishing a school history strengthens their sense of identity and pride.

Show Off Your School

Pride Power flourishes when students have an opportunity to host and conduct tours of their school for interested outsiders. Inviting business groups and senior citizens to visit the school promotes both school pride and positive public relations. Some schools find it beneficial to invite each local civic club to hold at least one meeting during the year in the school featuring a complimentary school lunch and a guided tour.

Interim Program of Mini-Courses

Many elementary and secondary schools across the nation find that conducting a series of mini-courses (between semesters, on Friday afternoons, etc.), can both broaden the curriculum and stimulate school spirit. When students feel their school offers something that other schools don't have, pride and loyalty are enhanced.

Before School Intramurals and Activities

Since many students arrive at school early, this time can often be utilized productively as a period for intramurals and other physical activities (e.g., volleyball tournaments, individual ping-pong contests, etc.). For some students this may be the best part of the day and can contribute significantly to their overall positive feelings about the school.

Follow Up Outstanding Graduates

Information about the achievements of outstanding graduates, celebrity alumni, and other successful former students is a valuable source of pride for current students. Inviting successful graduates to talk with students still in school promotes student appreciation of *their* school.

Faculty/Student Contests and Games

Almost any kind of faculty and student competition contributes to school spirit, excitement, and harmony.

Student Beautification Projects

Both elementary and secondary students have an increased sense of pride about their school when they are personally involved in some project (e.g., tree planting, maintaining a courtyard garden, painting murals, etc.), to beautify the building and grounds. Students are unlikely to vandalize property in which they feel some psychological investment.

All of the activities and projects described above and hundreds more like them help generate a constructive exuberance and enthusiasm among the student body that can turn around the tone of the school and work to reduce the occurrence of vandalism and violence in the school setting.

EFFECTIVE SCHOOL SECURITY PERSONNEL

As vandalism and violence increase, a new breed of personnel, the school security officer, has increasingly become a vital component of educational staffs across the nation. For many front-line administrators, the employment of effective security personnel is as important a consideration as obtaining competent teachers. More large high schools across the country now have some form of security personnel than do not. Some districts even find it necessary to employ full-time security directors as part of the central office staff. As long ago as 1976, Auroa, Colorado established a separate school security department within the administrative organization of the district.

A variety of patterns exist in providing security personnel. Sources for obtaining guards, monitors, etc., include:

- Agency contracts
- Off-duty police
- Additional directly employed personnel
- Criminology and police science students
- Deployment of night custodial staff

Although situations vary, the functions of school security personnel tend to be the same in most schools, as outlined below.

**TYPICAL DUTIES OF SCHOOL
SECURITY OFFICER**

- Patrolling and providing surveillance for building and grounds
- Checking halls, stairways, restrooms, parking lots, and entrances
- Identifying and interrogating visitors
- Monitoring bus loading and unloading
- Counseling/conferring with students regarding improper behavior
- Encouraging voluntary compliance with school rules
- Reporting to the school administration on problems and conditions affecting security

---

A better picture of the total role and responsibility of security staff in the school can be gained from the following sample position description of two different levels of security personnel.

**SAMPLE
JOB DESCRIPTION**

Name of position_____ Hall Monitor-High Schools _____

Position responsible to_____ Principal _____

Qualifications and skills necessary to perform this job satisfactorily:

Maintain good rapport with students and staff.
Effectively communicate with students and staff.
Be aware of the legal rights of individuals.

Duties and responsibilities of the position:

Exercise preventive measures to prevent delinquent acts.
Assist in the enforcement of school regulations.
Confer with building principals regarding students.
Give direction and assistance to students.
Exercise surveillance of unauthorized person and persons who loiter on school premises.
Assist at school functions when requested by building principals.
Assist in emergency situations when requested by building principals.
Perform other duties as may be assigned by building principals.

Sample Job Description

SENIOR HIGH SCHOOL SECURITY AIDE

Responsible to: Principal or Designee

Responsibilities:

General

1. become familiar with the school, the students, the staff and community
2. exercise preventive measures to reduce the possibility of delinquent acts or violations of school rules and regulations
3. confer with the principal and assistants in matters concerning the security of the building and grounds
4. give direction and assistance to students

Specific

1. provide supervision and protective security for the school building and grounds

2. assist in the enforcement of specified student regulations

3. exercise surveillance of unauthorized persons who loiter on school premises and report unusual cases to the principal or his or her designee

4. assist at school functions when requested and authorized to do so

5. assist in emergency situations

6. assist in the investigation of thefts, vandalism, and other violations upon request of the building administrators

7. regulate traffic and parking on school property

8. perform other duties and special assignments as directed by the building administrators

Special Requirements

1. maintain good rapport with students and staff, and effectively communicate with them

2. be cognizant of the legal rights of individuals

3. be qualified in first aid

4. be knowledgeable in all aspects of law enforcement, juvenile work, traffic control, alcohol drugs, investigation procedures, and human relations

5. shall not be uniformed or equipped with side arms

6. shall not usurp the disciplinary authority of certified personnel

7. shall not formulate school rules or regulations

Any administrator involved in initiating or implementing a program of security personnel should consider the following guidelines:

1. School security staff members do not have to be police, but they should be trained in police skills and investigative techniques.

2. Human relations training is essential for all security personnel.

3. Both sexes should be represented on the security force of any large secondary school.

4. Unless a desperate situation calls for desperate measures, school security officers can usually be most effective if they are unarmed, not in uniform, and "low key."

5. For optimum effectiveness, security personnel should become involved in school activities in a variety of roles. (In one high school, the hall monitor also serves as equipment manager, publicity director for the drama department, and advisor to the boys' cheerleading squad. In these roles, she has become one of the best-known and well-liked members of the entire school staff.)

One important caution should be noted in the establishment and utilization of a school security force. The employment of security officers may encourage teachers to abandon responsibility for student behavior outside their own classroom. (This result has already been encouraged by the collective bargaining agreements in some school systems.) This kind of situation can be disastrous. To be effective, the school security officer must be an integral member (but not the only member) of the school team committed to enforcing reasonable behavior standards.

STRATEGIES FOR REDUCING VANDALISM

In developing a comprehensive anti-vandalism campaign or plan, the administrator and school staff should bear in mind the following key points:

- Most vandalism occurs after school hours and on weekends. These times require special attention and extra precautions.

- Vandalism occurs in cycles. Anti-vandalism measures must be kept flexible. What works with one form of vandalism today may be inappropriate for a different form of defacing or destruction later on.

- Arson is the most costly form of vandalism. Measures of prevention, detection, and response in this area must receive top priority concern by the entire school staff.

- During the school day, the most volatile signal of potential vandalism is any gathering of class cutters, truants, and suspended students. (An additional ominous catalyst may be the presence of one or more unwanted intruders; e.g., dropouts, etc.). A fundamental principle of vandalism prevention must be diligent attention to attendance and tardiness policies and the dispersal of these potentially troublesome groups.

In selecting other effective approaches to curbing vandalism, teachers and administrators will find the following methods employed successfully in a variety of schools throughout the country to be both practical and productive.

Anti-Vandalism Action Steps

1. Conduct a *security audit* of all buildings and grounds.
2. Install locking hardware on all *interior* doors.
3. Chain crashbars on entrance doors whenever not in use and wherever safety codes permit. Entrances with panic exit equipment are known pushovers for vandals and thieves.
4. Install intrusion detectors/alarms (either motion or sound detectors can be effective). These may be audible on site, automatic telephone dialers, or wired direct to the police or a local monitoring station.
5. Install vandalism-resistant windows (plastic or other glazing). All glazing should be from the *inside*.
6. Establish an anti-vandalism incentive program. Schools have experienced some success both by making all or part of the building's unspent vandalism budget available for student use or by billing the student council directly for any deliberate destruction and allowing peer pressure to assume repayment to the council for such charges.
7. Require custodians to replace or repair any defacing or destruction as quickly as possible.
8. Install closed circuit TV or other electronic surveillance equipment on key areas such as:

   • main entrances
   • parking lots
   • computer rooms
   • service areas
   • music and theatrical storage areas
   • audio visual centers

This equipment serves as extra eyes for the security force and may be installed on a permanent basis if needed or set up temporarily during a sudden rash of unexpected acts of vandalism.

9. Lobby for adoption of municipal and/or state security codes similar to existing fire and safety requirements.

10. Arrange custodians' schedules to provide coverage for vulnerable areas during the nighttime and weekend hours.

11. Insist on a carefully followed *locking schedule* for all buildings. Some districts utilize solenoids and other electromagnetic devices to ensure proper locking.

12. Establish a student/citizen security advisory committee.

13. Eliminate anything climbable on building exteriors.

14. Provide adequate lighting for all vulnerable or frequently vandalized areas. Care must be taken to ensure that the lights themselves are as vandal-proof as possible.

15. Utilize onsite trailers rented on a low-cost basis to tenants willing to assume responsibility for monitoring and surveillance.

16. Eliminate interior student smoking areas wherever possible. These areas consistently serve as breeding grounds for a variety of destructive acts.

17. Create a Neighborhood Alert by informing residents in close proximity to the school of any vandalism problems and urging cooperation in apprehending offenders.

18. Encourage student art work and murals on all appropriate walls. (Hallways and stairwells particularly lend themselves to this kind of decorative display.)

19. Control community use and abuse of school facilities (see sample policy below):

(Sample Policy)

COMMUNITY USE
OF SCHOOL FACILITIES

A. Application for a school facility shall constitute acceptance by the applicant of the responsibilities stated and the willingness to comply with all rules and regulations regarding the use of school facilities as prescribed by the school district. The applicant must exercise the utmost care in the use of school premises and agree to protect, indemnify, and save harmless the district and its officers and employers of any and all claims, liabilities, and damages.

B. In the event of damage to school property, applicants shall accept the district's estimate of the amount of the same and shall pay all appropriate repair cost.

C. All organizations using school facilities shall provide an adult supervisor who shall remain with the group during all activities and be responsible for the group's conformance with all appropriate rules and regulations. The supervisor shall identify himself/herself to the custodian upon entering the building.

D. The individual named on the use permit and the group in whose name the permit is issued shall be held jointly responsible for any use to which a building is put under the permit granted and shall accept responsibility for any damage done to school property.

In spite of all of the precautions and preventive steps taken, some vandalism will occur in every school. When it does, administrators consistently find that the most effective course of corrective action is to require restitution. Making amends, which involves some work or personal sacrifice on the part of the offender, seems to have more impact as punishment than any form of reprimand, detention, or other routine disciplinary measure.

CHECKLIST FOR CURBING VIOLENCE

Violence is the most devastating discipline problem that can strike a school. It immobilizes morale and paralyzes positive action on the part of both students and staff. Unfortunately, there can be no question that incidents of violence have increased dramatically in the school setting over the past two decades. Recent studies show that while students are in school only about 25 percent of their waking hours, 35 to 40 percent of robberies and assaults involving students occur at or in schools. Of greater concern perhaps, is the fact that only a small portion of violent school acts are actually reported.

With this in mind, minimizing violence and erasing any climate of fear from the school must receive priority attention from all administrators and teachers. In order to understand the dynamics of school violence, the following insights have proved helpful to principals across the country: (1) disruptive acts are rarely planned; (2) crime and violence in schools usually do *not* center around student-adult conflict; (3) the people involved in violent situations normally do not want them to continue; (4) visibility and availability on the part of the school principal is a powerful deterrent to violence; and (5) an individual goal of all successful principals is to know potential disrupters personally. Personal relationships tend to reduce the risk of violence—this is particularly true where identifiable gangs exist within the school population.

When confronted with real or rumored situations involving violence, the following checklist offers practical approaches that can be followed in any school:

√ An official grapevine (network) of key communicators within the staff and student body can be invaluable in alerting the principal to potential flare-ups.

√ A program of Block Parents (homes identified by a window decal where harassed, frightened, or troubled students are encouraged to seek refuge) can reduce danger and restore confidence surrounding the school.

√ Well-planned "stakeouts by stakeholders" (parents, shop owners, etc.), during periods of stress can enable school officials to defuse embryonic incidents before any major outburst occurs.

√ The presence of youthful plainclothes men or women in the midst of a large secondary school often helps detect and correct explosive situations.

√ Snapshots, films, and video tapes of violent incidents provide the most convincing evidence to gain assertive parent and police cooperation.

√ Weapon control is essential. If the responsible administrator suspects the presence of weapons, the police should be called immediately.

√ Peer influence (bullies can also be peacemakers) and peer pressure (cancellation of important games, proms, etc.), can be effective tools in averting violence. It is essential, however, that school officials be willing to follow through. Never bluff where potential violence is concerned!

√ Every school should have a set of well-publicized (among the staff) formal emergency procedures. (See Sample Disturbances or Demonstration Procedures.)

√ Previous inservice training in first aid and CPR can be valuable assets in critical situations.

√ During periods of disturbance, an effective communication system (e.g., walkie-talkies, pocket beepers, etc.), among key staff members is essential.

√ One of the most disarming skills that building administrators can possess is knowledge/fluency in the language of one or more of the major ethnic-racial troups within the student population.

√ When violence erupts or is pending, every effort should be made to urge the local media to "cool it" and to avoid sensationalism.

√ If imminent danger exists, the principal or designee should not hesitate to employ one or more of the emergency tactical procedures below:

- Canceling all extracurricular events

- Shortening the school day

- Staggering the daily schedule, including opening and departure times. (It is sometimes prudent to time dismissal bells with the arrival of police cruisers.)

- Call a "cooling off" period (close the schools completely).

DISTURBANCES OR DEMONSTRATION PROCEDURES

Prevention of possible disturbances, through sound and relevant educational programs and open lines of communication with students, staff, parents, and community is essential and should be the prime concern of the entire community.

The principal is in complete charge of his or her building. A predesignated chain of command should be established in case of absence of the principal.

The following procedures should be considered in case of emergencies. The administrative staff should assess the situation to determine its seriousness and its effect on the safety of students and staff before taking any action:

A. **Put in effect the prearranged individual building emergency plan.**

B. **Notify an appropriate district office administrator of the situation.**

C. **Student Relations**

   1. Keep the students informed of the situation through normal channels of communication.

   2. Confer with student representatives of all groups representing all points of view in order to dispel rumors, calm fears, and provide as near normal operation as possible.

   3. Normal classroom operation should be maintained as much as possible and all students encouraged to stay in the classroom.

      a. No student should be physically restrained from leaving the classroom.

      b. If the disturbance is outside of the building, students should be kept away from windows.

      c. Students should be advised of the threat to their welfare that may be occasioned by leaving the room or building.

   4. No student or student group should be utilized in calming any disturbance that might place them in a situation where physical harm might occur or that would jeopardize their normal relationships with their fellow students.

D. **Staff**

   1. *Teaching Staff*

      a. Keep the teaching staff fully informed of the situation, using all available means of communication.

      b. Prearranged duties and responsibilities should be assigned.

      c. All teachers should record events that occur in

their vicinity with names, time, and place of events and action taken.

d. All teachers can have a calming effect by their actions and reactions to the situation. Good judgment and sound action will minimize any disturbance. Individual fears or emotions must be controlled and not communicated to students.

2. *Administrative Staff*

   a. Responsible to the building principal for performance of assigned duties.

3. *Custodial Staff*

   a. Responsible to building principal for assigned duties.

   b. Responsible for physical plant; i.e., utilities, fire alarm center, security of all entrances, etc.

4. *Clerical Staff*

   a. Safety of essential records without jeopardizing their own physical well-being.

   b. Minimize outgoing calls.

5. *Auxiliary Staff*

   a. All aides should remain at their assigned duties unless specifically assigned other duties by the administrative staff.

E. **Police Relations**

1. The building principal should alert the police for possible action.

2. The use of uniformed police in any crisis situation must be handled with extreme care. The principal should designate an entrance and room where uniformed police may enter and remain until called for duty.

F. **Community Relations**

1. *Parents*

   1. Keep parents fully informed of the situation by all possible means of communication.

   b. Organize a parent group that would voluntarily participate in attempts to calm disturbances in schools. A telephone chain should be established for speedy utilization of parents.

2. *Community Organizations and Leaders*

    a. Establish relations with organizations in the community and recognized community leaders so that they might be a resource for assistance in calming potentially dangerous situations.

G. **News Media Relations**

    1. Assign a staff person the specific responsibility of dealing with all news media.

    2. Provide a room for press conferences.

    3. Keep the news media informed of all decisions.

    4. Insist that news media personnel keep their cameras out of the building, or that they be brought to the press room.

H. **Closing of Schools**

    1. Only the superintendent of schools can legally authorize the closing of a school.

    2. If the decision to close a school is made:

        1. All neighboring schools should be informed.

        b. Parents will be informed as quickly as possible through designated communications media.

        c. Inform all students and staff.

        d. Staff will supervise dismissal.

        e. Bus transportation, if needed, should be arranged through the Director of Administrative Services.

This chapter has provided a variety of helpful hints for reducing vandalism and violence and establishing an atmosphere of order in the school. The next section contains practical advice for maintaining this order while observing all of the legal restrictions that increasingly challenge, confuse, and frustrate educators today.

5

How to Work Within The Legal Limits of Proper Disciplinary Action

Legal activism in the schools is on the uprise—particularly in regard to discipline. Educators at all levels find themselves increasingly uncomfortable in an age of legal limitations, litigation, and growing court regulations. While enrollments, budgets, and test scores are dramatically winding down, the number of court cases involving school personnel is consistently going up. As a result, teachers and administrators have become more and more tentative and timid in enforcing discipline at a time when some firmness, solidarity, and structure are desperately needed.

School authorities are beginning to question seriously whether the courts are friends or foes in maintaining order among students. On one hand, the courts are imposing ever expanding restrictions on school authority and action, while at the same time, withdrawing many of the traditional court-related support systems from discipline-minded school leaders. In what some professional educators call a "juvenile judge cop-out," a growing number of youth courts and court personnel (e.g., judges, referees, probation officers, etc.), have been criticized for the following faults:

a. A tendency to sidestep and refer discipline problems back to the school.

b. Actions that are often delayed or equivocal.

    c. Decisions that encourage students to consider themselves beyond traditional law and punishment.

    d. Refusal to deal with certain traditional areas of violation (e.g., truancy, smoking).

    e. Using school attendance as part of the penalty for student offenders.

While reducing efforts to back up schools in discipline cases, the local, state, and federal courts continue to hand down a litany of landmark decisions that constrain schools and leave educators bewildered as to what avenues remain open for enforcing school rules (see Landmark Cases Affecting Discipline below):

LANDMARK CASES AFFECTING DISCIPLINE

Case	Finding
Tinker vs. Des Moines School Board	Pupils do not shed their constitutional rights at the school door.
Wood vs. Strickland	School officials may be held personally liable if student rights are denied.
San Antonio Ind. District vs. Rodriquez	Education is a property interest under the 14th Amendment and cannot be denied without due process of law.
Gross vs. Lopez	Even a short-term suspension requires due-process provisions (e.g., a fair hearing).

    In Minnesota, a court action has further heightened the "paralysis of paranoia" affecting principals through a State Supreme Court decision in the Steven Larson vs. Jack Peterson case (Braham, MN, 1979). In this case, a 6-2 ruling found that an administrator can be held liable for a teacher's negligence if the administrator fails to meet supervisory duties outlined by district policy.

    Against such a backdrop of proliferating legal limitations, adverse court decisions, mushrooming lawsuits, and lack of court support, many educators are "running scared." They have become convinced that the schools and school personnel are powerless to enforce discipline. The problems these professionals recognize are real, but their conclusion is wrong.

Fortunately, knowledgeable and judicious school authorities can still maintain order, require respect, protect property, and punish pupils who disobey proper school rules—all within the law. The remainder of this chapter offers lasting, sensible advice for maintaining control while complying with all existing legal requirements.

STEPS TO ENSURE STUDENT RIGHTS/ RESPONSIBILITIES

There can be no question that student civil liberties have been dramatically redefined and enlarged by legislative and judicial fiat over the past two decades. As a consequence, school personnel must now pay expanded attention to a growing number of student rights and must treat all pupils as full citizens. At the same time, students cannot claim the school as a sanctuary from the conditions that accompany the rights of citizenship. In maintaining discipline, the charge to the school is to strike a balance between respect for the individual student's rights and the smooth functioning of the school for all students.

The status of student rights in today's society and today's schools is strikingly articulated in the following statement by Minnesota Commissioner of Education, Howard B. Casmey:*

A great number of evidences of the need for attention to student rights exhibit themselves in our changing society.

They include increased student restlessness and alienation; judicial emphasis on due process; the decision that the Constitution does not stop at the schoolhouse door; the emergence of a culturally distinct youth class—biologically and intellectually more mature than those of past generations; the growth of the universal demand for having a hand in the decisions which affect one's destiny; and the impact of the

---

*Minnesota State Department of Education (St. Paul) and National School Public Relations Association (Arlington, VA), *Emerging Rights of Students: The Minnesota Model for a Student Bill of Rights,* 1975, page 5.

Constitutional amendment which lowered the age of majority and therefore increased the status, as well as the numbers, of those who are now enfranchised.

All of these things—and more—emphasize that our schools should become more aware of (1) according students those rights which are mandated by law; (2) engaging in good, albeit not mandated, practices which have regard for the dignity of the individual student and which promote harmonious school/student relationships; and (3) promoting those activities which will lead students to understand that there are restrictions connected with individual rights and freedoms.

In developing discipline policies and enforcement procedures, the school staff must focus particular attention on student rights in the volatile areas listed below:

- Alcohol and drug abuse
- Dress and appearance
- Assembly or meetings
- Attendance
- Freedom of expression
- Corporal punishment
- Discrimination on the basis of age, sex, race, religion, marital status, handicap, etc.
- Search and seizure
- Student records
- Smoking
- Suspension, expulsion, and exclusion

One of the most helpful guides in protecting pupil civil liberties available to educators is the Minnesota State Department of Education handbook, *Emerging Rights of Students: The Minnesota Model for a Student Bill of Rights,* which contains the following specific implementation steps:

Recommendations for Preparation and Distribution of Student Rights Guidelines by Local School Districts

1. Seek wide input during the preparation of student rights policies, including feedback from students, teachers, administrators, community members and parents, attorneys, and agencies of local government.

2. Engage in legal research to assure that school district policies are consistent with emerging laws.

3. Review existing policies, including those that relate indirectly to student rights and conditions under which those rights may be exercised, to ensure parallelism.

4. Review school district policies to assure that they are updated.

5. Give careful consideration to brevity, clarity, and readability.

6. Distribute copies of school district policy to each student and parent or guardian (including transfer students and their parents).

7. Distribute copies of the policy to local news media, including television, radio, and newspapers.

8. Because titles and assignments differ among school personnel, the responsible authority for implementing student rights' guidelines must be spelled out clearly.

In considering and handling delicate discipline situations, teachers and administrators must maintain perspective by weighing any student rights involved against certain other court-tested rights—the rights of parents and the rights of the school itself (see below).

Parents have a right to—	*The school has a right to—*
• Preserve the individuality of their child.	• Establish reasonable rules.
• Expect safety.	• Deny illegal acts on school premises.
• Receive fair evaluations of their student.	• Prevent disorder.
• Property protection.	• Preserve an appropriate image of authority.
• An atmosphere conducive to learning.	• Define and maintain standards of behavior and expect parental cooperation.

The school's discipline program must take into account all of these rights. In most instances, the secret to avoiding a court contest over student rights is an *attitude* change. The staff must adopt a new sense of humaneness in treating pupils as persons and must eradicate any residue of past philosophy or practice that characterizes students as property or second-class citizens. Teachers and principals must not only recognize and honor the rights of students, but should realize that the knowledge of rights and responsibilities is an essential facet of every student's education. The effective school of today will have a master plan for encouraging students to accept increased responsibilities commensurate with their new found rights.

If school personnel follow the suggestions and safeguards outlined above, the current emphasis on broadened student freedom can become a tool for attaining better behavior through responsibility education. To maximize gains in school climate and to minimize problems, the professional staff should be cautioned, however, to seek legal counsel whenever there is any uncertainty about possible violations of student rights.

At the core of a successful and legal program of school control that respects student rights is an unflinching commitment to proper due process. The next section spells out clear-cut strategies for implementing necessary due-process procedures.

HOW TO "DO" DUE PROCESS

In order to operate within the legal bounds of appropriate disciplinary action, the principal and staff must share a primary concern for *procedural safeguards, equal protection,* and *unequivocal application of due process of law* to all students. Carefully following established due-process requirements may be somewhat burdensome and time consuming, but this should not serve as an excuse for failing to maintain firm standards of conduct.

In its most rudimentary form, the elements of proper due process are simply: notification, opportunity for hearing, and appeal provisions. In more complete terms, procedural due process requires that the following steps be taken in all discipline cases:

- All students shall be provided with complete and accurate information pertaining to all school policies, rules, and regulations.

- The student involved must be made fully aware of the specific matter(s) that have precipitated any proposed punishment or penalty.

- The student offender must have some opportunity to express his or her views regarding the incident(s) involved to a responsible authority.
- All decisions must be based on the incident or matters about which the pupil has been apprised.

To double-check compliance with due-process mandates, the school staff may find it helpful to review disciplinary procedures and actions in light of the questions below:

A. Was the rule, procedure, or order known to the student and was it one that would be considered reasonable and related to the necessary, orderly operation of the school?

B. Was the student notified relative to his or her behavior in this matter and was there prior knowledge and indication of probable disciplinary consequences for failure to comply?

C. Was there a fair, objective investigation of the circumstances and the facts prior to any disciplinary action and, in fact, was there a clear violation or disobedient act involved?

D. Is there specific information and documentation available to substantiate and verify the situation?

E. Does the disciplinary action taken reflect a degree that is consistent with the nature and seriousness of the offense?

F. Has the student's previous record been considered and has the student received treatment that is comparable and consistent with others who have been ·disciplined for similar circumstances?

If the answer to all of the questions above is yes, the staff need not fear adverse legal repercussions as a result of disciplinary action.

It should be noted that there are certain special due-process concerns relating to handicapped students. Recent federal legislation (e.g., P. L. 94-142) has clearly established the following inviolate rights for all handicapped or disabled pupils:

All handicapped students have a right to:

- an appropriate public education
- remain in the existing placement until any special education complaint is resolved

- an education in the least restrictive environment
- have all changes of placement effected in accord with prescribed procedures

This redefinition of handicapped pupils' entitlements may have some significant bearing on the handling of discipline cases involving these students. Any pupil dismissal action (suspension, expulsion, exclusion) against a handicapped student may be complicated by the requirements of this legislation.

Although some educators feel that due-process requirements place an undue additional burden on school personnel, many staffs find that implementing procedural due process helps in systemizing the disposition of discipline cases and in eliciting parental cooperation.

It may also be comforting for teachers and administrators to know that the elements of due process in school matters tend to be fewer and more informal than in other segments of society.

The basic concept that underlies current concerns for due process is simply *fairness*. This concept supposedly has always been the backbone of effective discipline practices in schools and so should not pose any insurmountable difficulties in its latest manifestation.

One area in which the rights of students and the necessity for due process has become particularly sensitive relates to the use, content, and confidentiality of pupil school records. The next section provides concrete help for handling discipline and other pupil records within existing legal requirements.

GUIDELINES FOR USING STUDENT RECORDS —THE PRIMACY OF PRIVACY

One of the most delicate aspects of modern-day discipline confronting school staffs is what to do about student records. Principals and teachers are torn, on the one hand, by the need to establish proper evidence and documentation of discipline actions in case of any eventual appeal or litigation, and on the other, by the importance of preserving pupil privacy. The perplexing question raised by many conscientious educators is simply, "What records of disciplinary infractions and penalties should be maintained and who should have access to such records?"

In any serious discipline situation, there is the clear possibility of legal action if the records are not handled properly. School personnel can be subject to personal liability if inappropriate release of information from any record causes a student embarrassment, loss of reputation, or other compensable loss. Two recent pieces of federal legislation have complicated the issue of confidentiality of pupil school records. These are—

1. Family Educational Rights and Privacy Act (Buckley Amendment)

2. Privacy Act of 1974

The purpose of these acts is laudatory in that they were designed to protect individual privacy and to enable citizens to gain access to personal records. The problem for schools stems from the fact that these purposes must be reconciled with the need to collect, maintain, and transmit appropriate school records so that the purposes of public education can be accomplished in a way that does not unduly jeopardize (in a legal sense) the professional lives and careers of the educational staff members involved. The capsulization below sorts out the legal essentials that educators must bear in mind in managing pupil discipline and other records.

Capsule Summary of Legal Requirements for Use of Student Records

- Every parent of a child subject to compulsory school attendance laws has the right of review of school records.

- Parents (or students) may challenge the accuracy of school records or portions of those records. (This doesn't mean that the school must change any record with which a parent disagrees.)

- If a request for a record change is refused, the parent or eligible student has the right to a hearing on the matter.

- If no change is made in a challenged record after a fair hearing, the parent or student has a right to a statement or rebuttal in the school records.

- A teacher's grade for a student cannot be challenged on the basis that it is unfair or reflects poor professional judgment.

- Appropriate school staff members, who fulfill a reasonable "need to know" criterion, have legal access to student records.

- Officials of another district to which a student is moving may also have access. (Notice of transmittal may need to be given to the student, parent, or guardian.)

- State/federal education agencies may have access to pupil records in the course of their authorized operation, but are required to maintain confidentiality.

- Material subject to a court order (subpoena) may be made available without consent (notification of the order, however, should be provided).

- Information requested by police officials and juvenile court personnel can be provided only with parental or pupil consent.

- Release of information to other outside parties can be made only with proper consent. (Use of a consent form is permissible and advisable, but a blanket consent is not appropriate.)

- Release of pupil directory information (e.g., census data, name, age, address, etc.), is permissible following proper public notice of attention via newspapers, announcements, etc.

- Some record of persons/agencies outside the school system requesting access to an individual's record must be maintained and made accessible to parents and students.

- All parents and students who have reached the age of majority should be formally apprised of the following rights:

  a. Right to be made aware of what records are kept

  b. Right of review

  c. Right to obtain a copy of any record (at the expense of the requesting party)

  d. Right to appropriate explanation and interpretation of any record

  e. Right to challenge

  f. Right to file a rebuttal

  g. Right to file a formal complaint if misuse of records is believed or suspected

In light of the legal limitations identified above, the best advice on managing records of discipline incidents and actions is to exercise these four precautions:

1. Keep complete personal notes regarding specific discipline situations for purposes of documentation, but do not include this information in the official school record.
2. Confine critical comments about students to specific incidents (avoid the use of any general derogatory terms).
3. Provide for the periodic review of all policies pertaining to record keeping and record retention.
4. Purge files of historic records that may be questionable under current conditions.

The purpose of most privacy legislation is to preserve individual citizen's personal and psychological autonomy. By adhering to the guidelines set forth in this chapter, educational personnel, at the same time, maintain the *school's autonomy* in handling discipline matters.

As an additional aid to school staffs, the sample policy below illustrates one model for assuring proper management of student discipline records.

(Sample Policy)

STUDENT RECORDS

Topeka (KS) Public Schools

It is the policy of the Board to assure that the welfare of each student is the chief criterion used in releasing information from student record files.

I. Responsibility for files

The principal or designated representative is responsible for maintaining and preserving the confidentiality of student records. All student record files shall be kept in a safe and secure place at all times.

II. Types of Files

The student record file consists of the pupil information record and the cumulative folder. The pupil information record constitutes the minimum personal data necessary for operating the educational system and is completed by the parent at the time of enrollment of each student. The cumulative folder additionally includes verified information such as standardized test data; clinical findings if applicable; health data; transcripts of academic work completed; grades; attendance; and date of graduation.

Note: Disciplinary records are considered supplementary and are not a part of permanent file.

III. Use of the Student Record

    A. The principal or designated representative may without consent of either the student or his/her parents or guardians release student records to the members of the district's professional staff who have a proper educational interest in examining the information.

    B. The student or the parent(s) or guardian having legal custody may inspect the individual personal records of the student at all reasonable times.

    C. A school official competent at interpreting student records shall be present to explain the meaning and implication of the records that are examined.

    D. The student, or the parent(s) or guardian having legal custody shall have the right to make written objections to any information contained in the records. Any written objection shall be signed and dated and it shall become part of the student's record.

    E. Upon the receipt of a written request from the student and/or the parent(s) or guardian having legal custody, the principal or his/her designee may grant permission for a third party to have access to the student's record.

    F. Any data found in a student's record file must be made available to any law enforcement officer or officer of any court upon presentation of a subpoena or court order.

IV. Transfer of Records

    A. When a student transfers to a school within the district, it shall be the responsibility of the principal or his/her designee to transmit the record data to the receiving school.

B. Records hand carried by students are not to be considered official files by the receiving school.

C. When a student transfers to a school not within the district, it will be the responsibility of the principal or his/her designee to transmit the record data to the Demographic Services Office.

D. To eliminate unnecessary or outdated information, a student's record shall be reviewed by the principal or his/her designee when the student moves from junior high to high school and when the student graduates.

E. At the time a student leaves Unified School District No. 501, the records shall be permanent and maintained by the Demographic Services Office for an indefinite period of time.

Although pupil record management is a sensitive, ongoing concern, a far more volatile issue revolves around the controversial use of corporal punishment in school discipline. Next is a common-sense look at the pros and cons of this long-debated practice.

SUCCESSFUL WAYS
TO HANDLE CORPORAL PUNISHMENT

For years, the most persistent and emotion-laden disagreement over school discipline practices has centered on the use and abuse of corporal punishment. The terms paddling, spanking, etc., immediately strike sparks of controversy in almost any school community.

Repeated polls show that a majority of teachers and parents do approve some use of corporal punishment for students. At the same time, the emergence of concerns over student rights, child abuse, and legal liability have intensified the polarization of views on the issue.

Despite the perpetual debate, the practice persists. In 1976-77, nearly 11,000 cases of corporal punishment were recorded in Indiana high schools alone—from these, 45 separate lawsuits ensued. As a result, some states and districts have passed laws banning the practice altogether. In other places, legislation has been enacted to legitimatize and protect the "use of the rod" in schools.

Some teachers would never consider use of corporal punishment and view it as an archaic and inhumane measure that has no place in an educational setting. Others feel helpless without the authority to use it and consider corporal punishment to be an absolute prerequisite for providing a proper school atmosphere.

The ultimate challenge to school practitioners and decision makers is to somehow neutralize the controversy over corporal punishment and to engineer an agreement over its use (or lack of it) among the disputants within their particular educational communities. Some districts find it both political and helpful to compromise by adopting policy that establishes the right to employ corporal punishment under certain circumstances, while at the same time, discouraging its use in actual practice.

In any event, experience across the country strongly indicates that the presence or absence of corporal punishment is *not* the critical factor in deciding the discipline fate of any school.

If some form of physical punishment is to be part of the school's discipline program, strict adherence to the simple Laundry List of Dos and Don'ts below is of utmost importance in any community.

A Laundry List of Dos and Don'ts on Corporal Punishment

DO	*DON'T*
• Check the law	• Use as a first line of punishment
• Consider community attitudes	• Ignore variables (age, sex, etc.)
• Describe punishable offenses	• Use for any offense caused by parental direction
• Define who will administer	• Administer with any inappropriate instrument

- Know where to paddle

- Have a witness

- Inform student of the reasons for punishment

- Obtain parent permission (in writing)

- Inform parents or guardians (in writing)

- Determine any exemptions (e.g., psychological or mental problems or other special situations)

- Permit the parent to veto

- File a report

- Administer to any vulnerable part of the body

- Use for purposes of spite, malice, or revenge

- Permit use by member of the opposite sex

- Use for off-campus incidents, except in very extreme situations

- Risk possible permanent injury

- Use unless the seriousness of the offense warrants

- Administer in anger

- Overuse

In addition to the Dos and Don'ts above, the three selected policy samples presented next demonstrate successful ways to provide for the reasonable exercise of corporal punishment in school discipline.

(Sample Policy)

CORPORAL PUNISHMENT

Oxnard (CA) Public Schools

The governing board of a school district may adopt rules and regulations authorizing teachers, principals, or other certified personnel to administer reasonable corporal punishment when such punishment is deemed an appropriate corrective measure....However, even when the governing board has adopted a policy of corporal punishment, such punishment shall not be administered to a student unless the student's parent or guardian has given written approval for such action....

At the beginning...of the regular school term, the governing board of a district that has adopted a policy of corporal punishment shall notify the parent or guardian that corporal punishment shall not be administered to a student without the prior written permission of the student's parent or guardian. The notice shall be a written notice and should be in a language that is understandable by the parent....

A teacher, vice-principal, or any other certificated employee of a school district shall not be subject to criminal prosecution for the exercise, during the performance of his or her duties, of the same degree of physical control over a student that the student's parent or guardian would be legally privileged to exercise. The degree of physical control that a certificated employee exercises shall not exceed the amount of physical control reasonably necessary to maintain order, protect property, protect the health and safety of students, or maintain proper and appropriate conditions conducive to learning....

(Sample Policy)

CORPORAL PUNISHMENT

Hillsboro (OR) Elementary School District

Physical punishment may be administered after less severe measures have not appeared effective and after the nature of the offense has been explained to the student.

Physical discipline is defined as spanking and shall be confined to the use of a paddle applied to the buttocks through the student's regular mode of dress.

Within the limitations of this policy, principals, teachers, and other certificated personnel may administer physical discipline with the following restrictions:

1. An oral or written report must be made to the parent or guardian following persistent violations of school rules by the student.

2. Physical discipline must be administered within the bounds of moderation and prudence; be suited to the gravity of the offense; and be administered with consideration of the physical condition and size of the student.

3. In all cases, physical discipline shall be free from the presence of other students.

4. Physical discipline shall be administered only in the presence of and with the permission of the building principal or department head or his/her designee.

5. The principal, or his/her designee is responsible for informing the parent or legal guardian of the administering of physical discipline. After physical discipline is administered, a report signed by the principal or person administering the punishment and by the witness must be placed on file as a matter of record.

A teacher or administrator is authorized to employ physical restraint when, in his or her professional judgment such restraint is necessary to prevent the student from doing harm to others or to self. When so employed, physical restraint shall not be considered a form of physical discipline.

(Sample Policy)

CORPORAL PUNISHMENT

Buffalo (MN) Independent School District #877

1. Policy

It is the policy of this school district to discourage the striking or hitting of a student.

2. Use of Physical Restraint or Force

The above is not intended, however, to preclude the use of reasonable physical restraint or force on the part of the teacher or administrator when necessary to maintain order and an effective learning climate within the school. Support staff in such cases are strongly discouraged to deal with students in a physical way. Support staff should seek the assistance of a certified staff member. The use of physical restraint or force is in order in the event that a teacher or an administrator:

    a. is subjected to the possibility of injury by a student.

    b. witness a physical disturbance between or among students.

c. deems it necessary to prevent physical injury to a student, students, or employees of the school district, or

d. deems it necessary to physically restrain or direct the movement or actions of a student in order to avoid undue disruption of the class-room or other area of the school environment.

With or without any formal policy guidelines, principals and teachers should always consider the following factors *prior* to administering any form of corporal punishment:

- severity of offense
- offender's age, size, health, etc.
- student's previous record
- alternative measures

Although corporal punishment is not inherently cruel and un-usual punishment, authority for its use is likewise not a sanction for any form of child abuse. When considering physical disciplin-ary action, school authorities should bear in mind the possible pitfalls of corporal punishment listed below.

Potential Pitfalls of Corporal Punishment

1. It may attack the person rather than the real problem.
2. It may produce adverse ramifications and side effects.
3. It may merely serve the needs of the adults involved and not the needs of the student.
4. Its effectiveness diminishes with use.

In using corporal punishment, as in all discipline action, the potential for legal reaction exists. The final segment of this chapter cuts through much of the myth and misunderstanding about educational lawsuits and offers concrete help for avoiding or successfully meeting legal challenges.

WHAT YOU SHOULD KNOW ABOUT LAWSUITS

It is obvious folly for school authorities to be unaware of how the law affects them, to pretend that litigation could never involve them, or to be naive enough to assume that the school always wins. It is equally foolish, however, to be paralyzed into disciplinary inaction out of fear of a possible lawsuit.

Even in today's era of free and easy litigation, most people who feel aggrieved still do not sue the school; and when they do, most malpractice and other suits filed against educational personnel are settled in favor of the school.

If due process has been followed and if teachers and administrators have done their job in the best interest of students, they should have no fear of lawsuits. In the unlikely event that some form of litigation does materialize, there is still no need for undue alarm. There are occasions when assertive legal involvement is both positive and helpful. The court may be a good arena in which school authorities can set needed precedents, establish certain standards that are lacking, and get some meaningful points across to students, parents, the public, and the judicial system itself. In any legal action, the key is for the school representatives to be able to demonstrate reasonableness of action and intent to serve the best interests of young people.

One basic preventionary step for school personnel is to become fully aware of current law and its impact on discipline. The school staff should take optimum advantage of all available resources including: (1) college courses on school law, (2) library legal references, (3) professional articles on legal issues, (4) advice and counsel from the district's school attorney, (5) legal advice available through professional organizations and associations, and (6) workshops and seminars treating legal concerns in the public sector.

Teachers and administrators should also be particularly mindful of the following high-risk areas that are most often vulnerable to discipline related lawsuits:

- denial of due process
- misuse of corporal punishment
- punishment involving academic penalties (e.g., withholding diplomas, lowering grades, etc.)
- slanderous or libelous statements about students
- disregard for or neglect of safety concerns

Other effective safeguards that may prevent possible lawsuits or prejudice the outcome of any court action in favor of the school include:

1. Provide prior notification of any rule change.

2. Avoid any distinctions based on sex, marital status, race, etc.

3. Maintain complete (personal) notes, records, and documentation of disciplinary incidents and actions.

4. Avoid any searches unless there is substantive cause to believe that illegal items are present and the student involved is permitted to witness the search.

5. Avoid any restriction on freedom of expression unless it interferes with school work and/or orderly class conduct.

6. Allow students to present petitions, testimony, and witnesses in their own behalf.

One final protection that school authorities should establish is adequate liability insurance coverage provided by the district. In some cases, it may be necessary to supplement this coverage through additional insurance available from many professional organizations at a nominal cost. Some administrators also find it prudent to negotiate a "hold harmless" clause in their master contract, which protects them from litigation that may occur after they have left the system and are no longer covered by district insurance. A sample "hold harmless" statement is included below.

(Sample Hold Harmless Clause)

St. Louis Park (MN) Public Schools

A. The School District agrees ... that it shall defend, hold harmless, and indemnify the administrator from any and all demands, claims, suits, actions, and legal proceedings brought against the administrator in his individual capacity, or in his official capacity as agent and employee of the School District, provided the incident arose while the administrator was acting within the scope of his employment and acting in good faith.

B. The School Board shall provide legal counsel and pay the fees for services rendered and costs advanced by such counsel in defense of the administrator, and shall pay any judgment which may be rendered against the administrators. In the event that a conflict exists as regards the defense to any claim between the legal position of the administrator and the legal position of the School District, the School District agrees to engage separate counsel for the administrator and the School District agrees to pay the fees for services rendered and costs advanced by such counsel. The School District further agrees that the choice of such separate counsel shall be made by the administrator and subject only to final approval by the School Board.

C. The School Board shall furnish such defense and pay such expenses and judgment only if the insurance carrier of the School District and the insurance carrier of the administrator, if any, declines to furnish the defense or pay such judgment or both.

D. Provision of counsel, payment of judgments, or any other costs or disbursements as provided herein, shall not be construed to render the School District liable for any claim, except as otherwise provided by law.

Despite the rampant paranoia that currently characterizes much of the thought in educational circles about the threat of court proceedings, it is possible to carry on a firm, fair, forceful, and effective discipline program without fear of judicial reprisals. By following the common-sense suggestions laid out in this chapter, school personnel can exercise their full authority and leadership in establishing a desirable school climate without exceeding any existing legal bounds.

One important aid to staying within the legal limits of proper disciplinary action is a well-defined set of legally sound district discipline policies. Chapter 6 sets forth a systematic approach to developing such policies, along with a sampling of successful, field-tested policy statements from representative districts in various parts of the country.

6

Steps to Establishing Effective Discipline Policies

Although successful discipline techniques can be employed by individual teachers and administrators, an overall district policy helps in mounting a uniform program of positive behavior management. Without such a policy, standards of behavior and enforcement procedures often become arbitrary and sporadic. A sound and simple policy statement provides school personnel with a consistent road map and action plan for preserving the proper learning environment. This chapter identifies the basic elements necessary for developing sound discipline policies and provides several model policies that are presently working in a variety of school districts.

TESTED TIPS FOR DESIGNING DISCIPLINE POLICIES WITH CLOUT

Developing a satisfactory general discipline policy is usually more important than the finished product itself. This process, accompanied by free and open publication of the results, serves as a powerful public relations strategy and as a tool for engaging public participation in a partnership for positive discipline in the schools. The steps below have proved productive in developing a workable school discipline policy statement for many differing districts:

- Multilevel involvement is fundamental to sound policy building. Meaningful dialogue and deliberation among students, staff, parents, and other community representatives are absolutely essential if the final policy is to reflect relevance and clout. The goal must be to arrive at a realistic consensus of behavior expectations and appropriate controls.

- The initial charge to any task force or group assigned to draft a policy should be to gather information regarding reasonable standards, existing patterns of behavior, problem areas, and acceptable enforcement procedures. To acquire this data, policy makers must talk directly to all parties to be affected by the final statement and must review school records related to school offenses.

- In order to streamline the process, efficient use should be made of such resources as existing policies in other districts and model statements available from commercial policy services (e.g., National School Board Association, Educational Research Services, etc.).

- An early decision must be made regarding the scope and bulk of the intended policy. In policy making, quality is always more important than quantity. A thorough and comprehensive statement of policy is a worthy goal, but no policy should strive to become the great American novel. An undue proliferation of rules often promotes inconsistency in administration and enforcement.

- Through the different stages of development, policy authors should keep their task in perspective by bearing in mind the following realities:
    - a. No policy can cover all contingencies.
    - b. No policy is a substitute for human and professional judgment.
    - c. No policy can completely satisfy all constituents.
    - d. No policy can be the final answer.

- Since policy language is no place for verbosity, cute phrases, jargon, or rambling rhetoric, consideration may need to be given to seeking assistance in the actual drafting and polishing of the proposed policy statement. Experienced policy makers, graduate students, and other communications specialists may be extremely helpful in achieving clarity and consistency in the final statement.

- Once drafted, public hearings or forums on the proposed policy should be conducted in order to broaden input and enhance acceptance before any official adoption takes place.

- Upon completion, the final policy should be widely circulated and openly publicized. Some districts find it beneficial to mail the adopted policy statement to all parents or residents and to include the policy on the school folder provided to every student at the beginning of each year.

- Policy development is an ongoing exercise. Ample provision should be made for the periodic review and updating of the final statement.

As a final test, it is wise to measure the school's official policy statement (in its final form) against the characteristics of sound policies outlined in the following section.

BENCHMARKS IN SUCCESSFUL POLICY MAKING

A careful review of existing discipline policies from a number of successful school districts reveals the common characteristics identified below. These features provide the criteria by which school personnel can measure the adequacy of any proposed policy statement:

1. The total statement should have a low *fog* index (e.g., crisp statements, simple sentences, monosyllabic language, minimum use of "educationese" and "legalese").

2. The successful policy takes into account the needs and attitudes of the entire school community and reflects agreed upon community standards to the extent possible.

3. The tone of the policy should accentuate the positive (e.g., *rights* are stressed as much or more than *responsibilities*).

4. The statement should include an appropriate emphasis on identifying and dealing with root problems—not just symptoms.

5. The policy should clearly define *discipline* as more than *punishment*.

6. All aspects of the policy must bear a real and substantial relationship to the lawful operation of the school district.

7. Adequate provision must be made for proper due process and the protection of all constitutional rights.

8. The policy should define, with reasonable clarity, all prohibited behavior.

9. To be complete, the statement should also spell out applicable corrective actions and consequences of performing prohibited acts.

10. For purposes of practical application, some policy makers find it advantageous to also distinguish between levels or categories of discipline offenses and penalties (see example below).

(Sample Discipline Categories)

Malad High School
Malad City, Idaho

I. *Major Role Violations*
   a. Attendance (forged excuses, etc.)
   b. Disrespect
   c. Drugs/alcohol
   d. Stealing ($10 or more)
   e. Vandalism ($10 or more)
   f. Willful disobedience
   g. Leaving campus without permission
   h. *Habitual* violation of petty or minor rules
   i. Tobacco

II. *Minor Rule Violations*
   a. Tardies
   b. Attendance (unexcused absence)
   c. Swearing
   d. Class interruptions
   e. Fighting
   f. Stealing (less than $10)
   g. Vandalism (less than $10)
   h. Cheating
   i. Necking
   j. Snowballing
   k. Loitering/horseplay in hall
   l. Unsatisfactory dress

>   m. Violation of individual classroom rules
>   n. Disruptive behavior that threatens safety or the well-being of staff, students, or facilities
> III. *Petty Rule Violations*
>   a. Horseplay
>   b. Litter

11. The policy should acknowledge the possibility of mitigating circumstances and provide some options or flexibility in these instances.

12. The focus of the policy should be on the consistent handling of each individual, but should not require that all students always be handled identically.

13. The policy should contain some disclaimer stressing that discipline is *not* the sole responsibility of the school.

14. The concept of self-discipline is emerging in many modern policy statements.

15. Some adequate mechanism for student grievance and redress is essential to a complete policy.

16. The policy should include steps to assure that the statement as finally approved is readily available to all interested and affected parties.

The descriptors above are frequent earmarks of an effective overall discipline policy. There is, however, one unique problem area that requires special policy attention because of the far reaching legal and personal ramifications involved. This sensitive area of *pupil exclusion* is discussed in detail in the next section.

SUGGESTIONS FOR HANDLING DISMISSAL, SUSPENSION, AND EXPULSION

Because of potential liability, school board members and authorities must strictly adhere to all legal requirements and due process provisions related to student dismissal. Repeated studies reveal a disproportionately high suspension rate for minority students in some parts of the country. Under this kind of cloud, school personnel cannot afford to be party to action that embodies any hint of violating student constitutional rights. Since federal interpretations are complex and state codes vary, legal counsel is a must in developing policies and procedures for pupil dismissal, suspension, or expulsion.

As a general guide, the elements that should be included in a sound dismissal policy are listed below:

1. *Complete definition of terms.* (E.g., expulsion, exclusion, hearing, etc.)

2. *Conditions/grounds for dismissal.* (The most commonly accepted grounds for any form of dismissal are: (a) willful violation of reasonable rules; (b) willful conduct disruptive to the education of others; and (c) willful conduct endangering health, safety, or property.)

3. *General guidelines for minimal due process.* (See Sample Guidelines below.)

(Sample Guidelines)

SUSPENSION AND EXPULSION GUIDELINES

Hillsboro Elementary School District
Hillsboro, Oregon

Special problems confront administrators and teachers in conducting educational programs free from disruption and free from the kinds of distracting behavior that impede the learning of any student. Occasionally, school officials may find it necessary to remove a student from school for a period of time as a disciplinary measure, or to provide time to develop a specific program or work out some satisfactory understanding with the parent. The guidelines are as follows:

• Fair treatment for all students shall be such as to protect them from arbitrary and unreasonable decisions.

• All disciplinary decisions affecting students shall be based on careful and reasoned investigation of the facts and the consistent application of rules and regulations.

• All students shall be informed of the school rules and procedures....These rules and regulations should be reviewed with the students annually, and a copy of this policy statement should be provided to new students upon enrollment in the school.

4. *Provision for full notification of all rights.* (Policy provisions should preclude any argument that parents or students were not fully informed of their rights regarding the exclusion process.)

5. *Step-by-step• hearing procedures.* (Proper conduct of any dismissal hearing is the most crucial phase of the expulsion/suspension process. Complete documentation of due process is essential for the record in case of any subsequent appeal or litigation. Steps must be taken to assure that whoever conducts the hearing cannot be accused of prejudging the case. See Sample Hearing Procedures, Sample Special Hearing Procedures, and Sample Suggestions of Hearing Officer selections below.)

(Sample Hearing Procedures)

**RECOMMENDED PROCEDURES FOR HEARING
ON EXPULSION OR EXCLUSION**

Independent School District #279
Osseo, Minnesota

- All hearings concerning long-term expulsion/exclusion of students from school shall be conducted by the school board or a committee thereof, or a duly appointed hearing officer at its regular meeting place, unless a different site is established in the hearing notice.
- The school board shall cause a record of the hearing to be made at its own expense.
- The superintendent shall have presented the presiding officer of the hearing with copies of all notices sent to the student and his parent or guardian, copies of all authoriza-

tion for release of the student's records in connection with the hearing, and the student's school records.

- The presiding officer of the hearing shall, after ruling that the recording procedures are satisfactory, conduct the hearing as follows:

    a. Call the hearing to order.

    b. Call the roll of all present and identify counsel, if present.

    c. Read the charges and mark exhibits and receive them in evidence.

    d. Call upon the school representatives to present evidence substantiating the charges, including written documentation and witnesses.

    e. Call upon the student or spokesman to question any witnesses presented by the school district after each witness has testified.

    f. Call upon the student or spokesman to present documentation and witnesses on behalf of the student.

    g. Permit the school representative to question any witness on behalf of the student, immediately after the witness has testified.

    h. Call upon the school representative to summarize the case against the student.

    i. Call upon the student or spokesman to summarize the case for the student.

    j. Adjourn the hearing.

    k. The hearing officer, committee, or board shall deliberately write findings of fact and determine the recommendations to be made to the school board.

- The student and his parent or guardian are entitled to a representative who may be an attorney. The school board may appoint an attorney to present the evidence on behalf of the school district.

- If the spokesman for the student be other than the student or his parent or guardian, such spokesman must have written authorization from the student, parent, or guardian in order to view the student's record or obtain copies thereof.

- The hearing officer or hearing board shall make findings of fact, recommend action to the school board ... the school board shall take action on the findings and recommend action ... and instruct the clerk of the board to send to the student and parent or guardian within 48 hours after the decision is rendered. Copies will be sent simultaneously to the school board, the student, and his parent or guardian and his counsel, if one is involved.

- A copy of the hearing record will be made available to the student or his parent or guardian or representative, in transcript form, as determined by the school board upon request and without charge.

(Sample Special Hearing Procedure)

OXNARD (CALIFORNIA) SCHOOL DISTRICT

USE OF INTERPRETER

The hearing and presentation of evidence shall be conducted in the English language. The proponent of any testimony to be offered by a party to the hearing who does not proficiently speak the English language shall provide an interpreter approved by the president of the school board or other body conducting the proceeding, as proficient in the English language and the language in which the witness will testify, to serve as interpreter during the hearing.

The cost of the interpreter shall be paid by the district if the board finds that the pupil or his/her family cannot reasonably afford the cost of an interpreter, but otherwise the cost of such an interpreter must be paid by the party providing the interpreter....The district may, in lieu of hiring an interpreter, make available an employee of the district proficient in the language in question. Interpreters shall be used only to translate the proceedings for hearing participants.

*(Sample Suggestions
for Hearing Officer Selection)*

**RECOMMENDATIONS FOR THE SELECTION
OF A HEARING OFFICER**

Independent School District #279
Osseo, Minnesota

- Although the entire school board is empowered to conduct the hearing, it is recommended that the board appoint a hearing officer.
- The hearing officer should be a neutral individual in the case with a reputation for sound common sense and fair treatment of all parties.
- The ideal situation would be to have available in the area an experienced individual, preferably not from the local community.
- A member or committee of the school board may also conduct the hearing.
- The hearing officer should not be anyone presently connected with the juvenile court and judicial system or law enforcement agencies.
- The function of the hearing officer is to determine what is fact, and on the basis of that make a recommendation to the school board for action. The hearing officer's recommendation may or may not coincide with that of the school's administrative personnel and the school board's decision may or may not follow the recommendation of the hearing officer.

6. *A complete system of documentation/recordkeeping.* (The next few pages contain sample forms and records that have proved helpful in facilitating and documenting the student exclusion process.)

(Sample Form)

REPORT OF PUPIL SUSPENSION

Oxnard (Calif.) School District

To _____   _____
             Parent or Guardian   Address

Name of Pupil _____ Birthdate _____

Grade _____

is suspended from _____School for _____

days.

The pupil is entitled to return to school on _____

Time _____.

Statement of specific charges: _____

_____

You are requested to attend a meeting on _____

_____ _____ _____ _____
   Time   Date   Signature   Title

(Sample Form)

NOTICE OF SHORT-TERM SUSPENSION

Edmonds School District #15
Lynwood, WA

Student's Name _____ Grade _____

Parent/Guardian's Name _____

Address _____ Phone _____

You are hereby notified that you have violated the following
school district rule(s):

You have violated the above by the following action(s) on or
about the time(s) and place(s) cited here as determined by
the specific evidence:

The corrective action or punishment to be imposed shall be
suspension from school as follows:

Date this _____ day of _____ 19____

_____   _____
Student Signature   School Admn. Signature
(acknowledging receipt only)

_____   _____   _____
Parent/Guardian Signature   Date   School
(acknowledging receipt only)

(Sample Form)

Certified Mail

**NOTICE OF DISCIPLINARY HEARING BEFORE THE
OXNARD SCHOOL DISTRICT BOARD OF TRUSTEES TO
CONSIDER THE EXPULSION OF** _____

Oxnard (CA) School District

It has been recommended to the Board of Trustees by the Superintendent that _____ be expelled from school. Please be advised that a hearing upon this matter will be held in executive session before the Board of Trustees at the Oxnard School District, located at _____ at _____ p.m. on Wednesday, the _____ day of _____, 19____.

The basis for this proposed action are the following charges:

- Caused damage to school property
- Engaged in habitual profanity
- Threatened to cause physical injury to another person
- Willfully defied the valid authority of teachers and administration

Witnesses to be called include _____
_____
and any other witness not known at this date.

(Sample Form)

REPORT OF HEARING OFFICER

Osseo (MN) Public Schools

_____
                                    Date

Re:_____
                    Name of student

A hearing was conducted before me on _____
                                                            Date

at _____ at _____
        Time   Location

relative to the proposed _____
                                    Exclusion/Expulsion

of the above named student.

The facts found are as follows:

I recommend the following action:

_____
                        Hearing Officer or
                        Presiding Officer

(Sample Form)

Oxnard (CA) School District

STATEMENT OF FINDINGS OF FACT BY THE BOARD OF
TRUSTEES IN THE EXPULSION HEARING OF _____

HELD AT _____ **P.M. ON** _____

After having heard the testimony presented and having given _____
and his parent an opportunity to comment on the testimony and based on _____
statement that all statements made by the witnesses are true, we have found _____
guilty of the following acts:

- Caused damage to school property
- Caused physical injury to another person
- Engaged in habitual profanity
- Disrupted school activities

Therefore, the Board of Trustees determines that _____ be expelled from the District for the balance of this school year.

Dated this _____ day of _____.

_____
President,
Board of Trustees

_____
Clerk, Board of Trustees

(Sample Timeline)

EXPULSION TIMELINE

Oxnard (CA) School District

- Within *20 school days/25 school days: schedule expulsion hearing.* An expulsion hearing shall be held within 20 school days of the date expulsion is recommended or within 25 school days of the date suspension is ordered for the offense, whichever is sooner, unless the pupil or the pupil's parent or guardian request in writing that the hearing be postponed....

- *At least ten days prior to the date of the hearing ... notification of expulsion hearing.*

- *Five school days prior to the date of expulsion: pupil, parent or guardian request for a public hearing.*

- *Five school days: duration of expulsion hearing.*

- *Within three school days following hearing by hearing officer or administrative panel: recommendation on expulsion presented to the governing board.*

- *Within 35 school days/40 school days: deadline for expulsion by the board.* A decision of the governing board whether to expel a pupil shall be made within 35 school days of the date expulsion is recommended by a principal or within 40 school days of the date suspension is ordered for the offense, whichever is sooner, unless the pupil or the pupil's parent or guardian requests in writing that such a decision be postponed.

- *Within 30 days: file notice of appeal.*

- *Within five days: service of notice of appeal and rules.*

- *Within ten days: filing of transcript.* Within ten days after service of notice of appeal, the pupil, parent, or guardian shall file with the County Board of Education a written verbatim transcript of the entire hearing from which the appeal is taken.

- *Within ten days: Dismissal of Hearing.* If the pupil, parent or guardian should fail to file a transcript or agreed statement of facts within ten days, the Board shall dismiss the appeal for lack of prosecution.

- *Within ten days: filing of documentation by the district.*

- *After record on appeal is filed.* After it is filed with the Board, the record on appeal shall be available for inspection by the pupil, parent, or guardian, and the district and their respective representatives, if any, at all reasonable times.

- *Within 20 days: setting hearing on appeal.*

- *As soon as practical and in no event less than ten days before the date for which the hearing is set:* The board

> shall serve written notice of the hearing upon the pupil, parent, or guardian and the district as soon as practical and in no event less than ten days before the date for which the hearing is set.
>
> • *At least five days before the hearing.* Request by the pupil, parent, or guardian that the hearing be a public hearing.
>
> • *Continuance of Hearing Date.* When the parent, pupil, or guardian and the district jointly seek a continuance to a later agreed upon date, the board shall reset the hearing date to the date specified in the written request or to a date as soon thereafter as the matter can be reasonably heard.
>
> • *Ten days:* limit of continuance....
>
> • *Within three school days: decision by County Board.*

7. *A specific timeline sequence of dismissal actions.* (See Sample Timeline.)

8. *A specific statement of the duration/limitations of suspension or expulsion (usually prescribed by law).*

9. *Some clear identification of the responsible party or parties for each step in the dismissal process.*

10. *Well-defined provisions for appeal.*

11. *A definite procedure for readmission.* The readmission procedure should be designed to minimize the damaging effects of exclusion and may include: (a) a hearing where the student can demonstrate a change of attitude or behavior; (b) an opportunity for witnesses to appear in behalf of the student; and (c) an agreement to discount past behavior and provide the student with a "clean slate".

All the steps and procedures outlined above will assist the school to expedite pupil exclusion when necessary. It should be stressed, however, that dismissal in any form should be a last-resort measure in maintaining positive discipline. It is far more important that the school's first line of defense be an active concentration on the prevention of dismissal through the early detection of behavior problems.

At best, student suspension or expulsion is negative and nonproductive in that it offers minimal opportunity for behavior modification while denying the student access to a regular and meaningful educational program. Exclusion should be used only when a student poses a direct or serious threat to people or property. In all other instances, every effort should be made to take some alternative course of action for lesser offenses. One alternative strategy that has worked successfully in numerous schools across the country is the introduction of some form of *in-house suspension*, whereby the student is retained in the school, but isolated from sources and targets of disruption. A program of in-house suspension offers the following advantages:

- The student does not miss out on necessary regular assignments.
- The suspension period is not a vacation for the student.
- The student remains under proper professional supervision.
- The school does not transfer its problem outside to the community at large.

Regardless of whether traditional exclusion or some program of in-house suspension is utilized as a disciplinary measure, the school continues to be responsible for the education of the pupil during the dismissal period.

As a final help to school personnel in establishing a complete set of effective discipline policies, the next section contains a representative collection of model policies that may be adopted or adapted in most school settings.

SAMPLE DISCIPLINE POLICIES THAT WORK

The abbreviated sample policies that follow reflect a variety of workable discipline statements that have been applied in successful school districts, large and small. The sampling is not intended to be exhaustive; but rather to offer a cross section of actual policy statements that deal with the fundamental areas necessary for discipline.

(Sample Policy)

DISCIPLINE POLICY PHILOSOPHY

White Bear Lake Public Schools
White Bear Lake, MN

The school is a community of people who live and learn together, where each person has individual rights and responsibilities. It is necessary that the school provide constructive, formative experiences which develop positive attitudes for learning, leading to self-direction, responsibility, and community concern. To enable the school to function effectively, there is a need for clear policies and procedures which outline a framework in which people can learn in an atmosphere of trust and mutual respect. These policies are intended to develop within the individual a sense of good judgment consistent with a desirable system of values leading to proper self-control and self-direction.

Every individual throughout the school system must take a personal and active responsibility for discipline. Discipline begins in the home between the parent and child. Discipline continues in the classroom with the relationship between the teacher and pupil. Parents are expected to send their children to school in the proper state of health and to support the school discipline code. The school staff is expected to work with students in a fair, firm, and friendly manner and to hold students accountable to individual school discipline codes....

(Sample Policy)

Topeka (KS) Public Schools

OUR PHILOSOPHY OF DISCIPLINE

I. *Basic nature of discipline*—Good discipline is usually positive rather than negative in nature. It is the result of keeping pupils interested and actively engaged in constructive and worthwhile learning activities, rather than punishing pupils for doing things which are destructive and antisocial. The purpose of discipline is to help the pupil to develop self-control with due respect for authority.

II. *Importance of good discipline*—Good discipline in the schools is extremely important to the whole community, but particularly important to pupils, teachers, principals, superintendents, boards of education, and parents. In the end, good discipline is important to the educational process, for it is a vital factor influencing the kind of schooling pupils will receive.

III. *Discipline procedures must be in accordance with good educational practices and due process*—The Board of Education must know that the procedures relating to discipline are in accordance with good educational practices and due process in order to give the support that teachers and administrators need.

IV. *Punishment is sometimes necessary*—It is the firm belief of the board that the large majority of pupils are well behaved, industrious, and eager to learn. The taxpayer's money and the school's efforts should not be misspent by permitting the few unruly pupils to waste time, upset classes, and distract others who wish to learn. For the small percent of pupils who do not respond to a positive approach, punishment of some kind is sometimes necessary. When involving punishment or restraint, good discipline should be fair, dignified, and administered without anger or malice.

(Sample Policy)

STUDENT EXPECTATIONS

Mastick School
Alameda (CA) Unified School District

We are all unique and special at Mastick School.

We like to see others happy and ourselves happy.

We respect the rights of other students and adults in the school.

We understand that we are in school to learn.

We understand that teachers are in charge.

OUR HUMAN RIGHTS

I have a right to be happy and to be treated with kindness at school.

* * * * * *

I have a right to be safe at this school.

* * * * * *

I have a right to hear and be heard at this school.

* * * * * *

I have a right to learn in a clean and healthy school.

* * * * * *

I have a right as an individual to express my feelings and opinions as long as they do not interfere with the rights of others.

(Sample Policy)

PREAMBLE

East Allen County Schools
New Haven, Indiana

The East Allen County Schools, believing that the democratic way of life contributes the most benefit and happiness to members of society generally, the school, as an agency of society, should then be dedicated to the development, improvement and preservation of all democratic ideals. Further, the rights and responsibilities of the individual and the legal processes, whereby necessary changes are brought about, are primary concerns of the East Allen County Schools.

The school is a community and the rules and regulations of a school are the laws of that community. All those enjoying the rights of citizenship in a school community must also accept the responsibilities of citizenship. A basic responsibility of those who enjoy the rights of citizenship is to respect the laws of the community.

(Sample Policy)

PARENT RESPONSIBILITIES

David Douglas (Oregon) School District

- Send your child to school as requested by Oregon School law.
- Make certain your child's attendance at school is regular and punctual and all absences are properly excused.
- Insist that your child is clean, dressed in compliance with school rules of sanitation and safety, and in a fashion that will not disrupt classroom procedures.
- Be sure your child is free of any communicable disease and is in as good health as possible.
- Guide your child from the earliest years to develop socially acceptable standards of behavior, to exercise self-control, and to be accountable....
- Teach your child, by word and example, respect for law, for the authority of the school, and for the rights and property of others.
- Know and understand the rules your child is expected to observe at school; be aware of the consequences for violations of these rules and accept legal responsibility for your child's actions.
- Instill in your child a desire to learn; encourage respect for honest work and an interest in exploring broader fields of knowledge.
- Become acquainted with your child's school, its staff, curriculum, and activities. Attend parent-teacher conferences and school functions.

(Sample Policy)

South Washington County Schools
Cottage Grove, MN

Rights and Responsibilities: A prized birthright of state citizens is that of an education at public expense for those citizens between the ages of 5 and 21 unless they graduate from high school before the age of 21. The birthright carries with it correlative responsibilities as it applies to the maturation of students as follows:

IT IS THE STUDENT'S RIGHT TO:	IT IS THE STUDENT'S RESPONSIBILITY TO:
Attend school in the district in which his/her parents or legal guardians reside.	Attend school daily, except when properly excused, and to be on time to all classes.
Attend school until graduation from high school at public expense.	Attend school until 16.
Assist in making of decisions affecting his/her life in school.	Pursue and attempt to complete the course of study prescribed by the state and local authorities.
Express his/her opinions verbally or in writing.	Express his/her opinions and ideas in a respectful manner, so as not to offend or slander others.
Expect that the school will be a safe place for all students to gain an education.	Be aware of all rules and regulations for student behavior and conduct himself/herself in accordance with them.
Dress in such a way as to express his/her personality.	Dress and appear so as to meet fair standards of propriety, safety, health, and good taste.
File a grievance with the appropriate school official when accused of misconduct.	Be willing to volunteer information in disciplinary cases should he/she have knowledge of importance.

Be afforded a fair hearing with the opportunity to call witnesses in his/her own behalf and to appeal his/her case in event of disciplinary action.

Be willing to volunteer information and cooperate with school staff in disciplinary cases.

Expect that where he/she bears witness in a disciplinary case, his/her anonymity will be honored by the school.

Assist the school staff in running a safe school for all students enrolled therein.

Be represented by an active student government selected by free school elections.

Take an active part in school life. Run for office. Vote for the best candidates. Make problems known through representatives.

Assist in making of school rules.

Assume that until a rule is waived, altered, or repealed, that it is in full effect.

(Sample Policy)

North St. Paul-Maplewood (MN) Schools

STANDARDS OF CONDUCT

The following conduct has been determined to be unacceptable:

- Class truancy
- Cheating
- Abusive language
- Class disruptions
- Out-of-class disruptions
- Insubordination
- Threats
- Self-inflicted injury
- Distribution of alcohol or other drugs
- Truancy from premises
- Off-limit violations
- Bomb threats
- False fire alarms
- Trespassing
- Gambling

- Assault to student
- Assault to school employee
- Vandalism
- Theft
- Possession of stolen property
- Possession and furnishing of tobacco
- Use of tobacco
- Possession of alcohol and other drugs
- Use or under the influence of alcohol and other drugs

- Interference/obstruction
- Inappropriate student attire
- Unauthorized use of school property
- Reckless/careless driving
- Parking in prohibited areas
- Locker violations
- Tardiness
- Statutory crimes
- Violation of bus safety codes

(Sample Policy)

Ames (IA) Community School District

I. Authorized Actions: The following actions are authorized ... and may be taken at any stage in the discipline proceedings:

A. By the teacher or principal or designee:
1. Detention, before or after school
2. Remove from class, not to exceed one day

B. By the principal or designee:
1. Denial of privileges and/or participation in extra-curricular activities
2. Probation
3. In-school suspension
4. Suspension

C. By the principal:
1. Removal from specific class for the balance of

> the semester, with prescribed home study or educational alternative
> D. By the board of directors:
>   1. Expulsion

(Sample Policy)

Mora (MN) Public Schools

JUNIOR HIGH DISCIPLINE POLICY: MERIT-DEMERIT PROGRAM

Discipline is the responsibility of the individual student.... This system attempts to reject negative behavior and not the student. The demerit scale and guidelines noted below are a means of recording misbehavior, and will be used in arriving at a nine-week conduct grade for all junior high students. Receiving demerits for misconduct is not a punishment, but merely a record or grade similar to the grades one receives in an academic class....

The following demerits scale is for the nine-week reporting period. A cumulative count will begin the first of each reporting period and will be the basis for a conduct grade at the end of the reporting period....

Demerits	Grade
0-4	S+
5-9	S
10-19	S

(letters forwarded to parents on 15th demerit)

20-30	U

(Automatic 1 day suspension for any demerits over 30)
(1 hour of detention at 20+ letter)
(2 hours of detention at 25+ letter)

Guidelines

In order to establish consistency in giving demerits the following will be used:

No. of Demerits

1.   2   Leaving cafeteria, detention...in unsatisfactory condition

2.	1	Taking food from cafeteria
3.	3	Loitering in the school....
4.	2	Coming to class unprepared
5.	2	Excessive tardiness
6.	2	Having no pass
7.	1	Use of gum during school hours
8.	2	Inappropriate dress, per incident
9.	3	Leaving library or class without permission
10.	4	Misconduct—in cafeteria, library
11.	5	Inappropriate public display of affection
12.	6	Use of profanity
13.	6	Unauthorized presence in school
14.	5	Possession of cigarettes
15.	10	Possession of drugs
16.	10	Smoking in school
17.	11	Possession of any item (guns, knives, fireworks, etc.), that is illegal
18.	15	Use of items in number 14
19.	2-14	Truancy—2 demerits for each hour
20.	6-10	Insubordination...
21.	10	Fighting
22.	4	Leaving school grounds without permission
23.	6	Cheating (per offense)
24.	15	Assault
25.	10	Stealing
26.	15	Willful destruction of school property...
27.	15	Use of alcohol...
28.	15	Extortion or intimidation of others...
29.	4-15	Disciplinary problems of highly severe nature not included above

The following sample of the demerit slip will be filled out and signed by the teacher and the demerit stub given to the student. Should the student elect not to accept the stub, the teacher should make a note of this and send it along with the demerit slip. There will be no excuse, however, for a student not knowing how many demerits he (or she) has.

DEMERIT SLIP

Last Name _____ First _____ Middle _____

Date _____ Grade _____

_____ Demerits

Reason: _____

_____

Teacher's Signature _____

(Sample Policy)

Albuquerque (NM) Board of Education

Grievance Procedure

It is the intent of the board that students and their parents should be informed of the regulations regarding disciplinary and other procedures affecting students within the school. To this end, faculties, parents, and students shall attempt resolution of problems affecting students and the educational process by informal means. However, any student or parent who feels that the conditions of the school, or a decision made by its staff are not fair or responsible, shall be afforded a meeting with the principal or his/her designee to discuss the matter. If the student or parent is not satisfied, he/she shall be afforded the opportunity to confer with the area superintendent regarding the matter. From the decision of the area superintendent, the student or parent may appeal to the office of the district superintendent and subsequently to the board of education if not satisfied with the disposition of the matter.

The information and illustrations contained in this chapter provide a solid framework within which any school or district can develop a sound set of discipline policies. Such policies are important road maps and action plans in assisting the school to maintain a productive order-oriented environment. Ultimately, however, it is people—not policy—who make the real difference in discipline. All of the central actors involved in the school must form a commitment to ensure a safe and secure setting for student growth, if good discipline is to prevail. Unfortunately, one of the most influential components of this coalition, the parent public, is often overlooked in the formation of a positive discipline program.

The next chapter offers concrete help for actively engaging parents as partners in the school's quest for better behavior.

7

Using Parents as Partners for Positive Discipline

In managing and maintaining proper discipline in the school, the pivotal influence of parents is often overlooked or misjudged. In most difficult discipline situations, the family (particularly the parents) may be either an integral part of the problem or a welcome part of the answer. One of the most severe tactical errors that school officials can make is to ignore or misuse the potential of *parent power* for supplementing, supporting, and cementing the school's efforts to establish positive behavior.

When the school is in trouble, the most logical source of assistance lies with the parent community. To engage parents effectively in a partnership for better school climate, most staffs must overcome three intrinsic obstacles:

1. parental fear/discomfort in dealing with authority (e.g., teachers and administrators);

2. the eternal tendency for parents to evaluate the school on the basis of their own experience in times of dramatic change;

3. the conviction on the part of both parents and teachers that they know what's best for the children.

To neutralize these inhibiting forces, the school's program of parent outreach must be based on truth, trust, and belief that mom and dad truly have a legitimate role to play in school discipline. The following sections present a potpourri of suggestions for successfully forging a bond between the home and the school in behalf of better behavior.

HOW TO ASSURE SUPPORT
THROUGH THE PARENT TEAM CONCEPT

Some school staffs compound their behavior problems by consciously or unwittingly forming an unholy alliance against the necessary and valid interests of parents. Such schools are characterized by insensitivity, cynicism, and callous disregard of parents in a belief that "the less they know the better."

Where discipline is best, school personnel welcome and encourage the partnership of parents. More than the school, the home is usually the real citadel of caring/concern for kids. It is foolish for teachers and administrators to bypass the powerful help that is available from the parent-as-ally.

To ensure optimum collaboration between the home and the school, the staff should endorse and energetically promote a *Parent Team Concept*. Under this approach, parents, teachers, and administrators become collegial stakeholders in the pursuit of educational excellence and responsible student behavior. This concept is predicated on joint action and efforts to achieve these common goals through sensitive consideration of the needs of the students, the parents, and the school. Thus, teachers and parents serve as co-advocates for the children. The essential elements of a productive Parent Team program are illustrated in the *Partnership Wheel* (Figure 7-1).

Once fully activated, the Parent Team concept can pinpoint a host of things that parents can do for and with the school to upgrade discipline, including the following examples:

- volunteer supervisions (to and from school, on playgrounds, in lunchroom, etc.)
- model healthy conduct

- provide block homes
- get others involved
- serve as observers for surveillance and reporting
- reinforce positive behavior
- spot problems early
- provide feedback
- set the record straight in the community

PARTNERSHIP WHEEL

(Characteristics of an Effective
School-Parent Team)

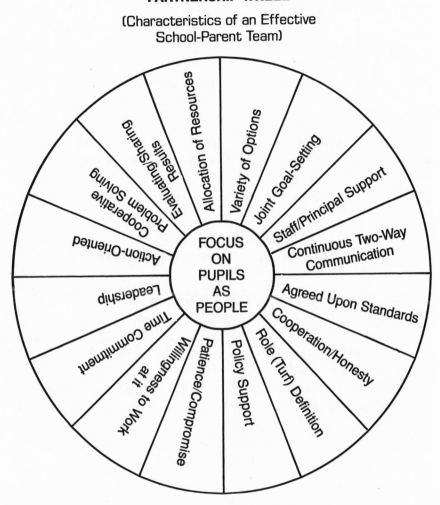

Figure 7-1

The five preliminary steps below can ease the way in introducing a workable Parent Team approach for solving discipline problems in any school:

1. Stress the importance of *every* staff member being available, credible, professional, and understanding in all parent dealings.

2. Conduct a community publicity campaign to boost discipline.

3. Inform parents that they are expected to punish students for wrongdoing (parents need to know that the school wants them to manage their own turf).

4. Use contracts between the parent and the child as one alternative approach to discipline.

5. Expand the Parent Team to include everyone involved in the life of the student (e.g., grandparents, babysitters, ministers, scout leaders, etc.).

Ultimately, the crux of the Parent Team relationship rests on the quality of the communication that flows both ways between home and school. The next section details a variety of positive, practical, and pretested means for improving this communication.

PRACTICAL STEPS
FOR COMMUNICATING WITH PARENTS

Repeated studies show that parents want to know more about what's happening in school, what the problems are, what's being done about them, and how they can help. It is in the best interest of the school to provide this information through the most effective means possible. If its efforts are earnest and its communications are honest, the school *will have* the necessary parent and public support to carry out any reasonable discipline program.

The primary hazards to effective communication back and forth between the school and the home include:

A. Nonspecific content

B. Communication overkill

C. Mixed messages

D. Overemphasis on negative aspects

E. Too many links in the chain

F. Status intimidation

G. Failure to keep the audience in mind

H. Overuse of "educationese" (many professionals become "jargon junkies" because they are inexperienced, suffer from insecurity, want to impress and/or strive to avoid hurt feelings)

The suggestions below zero in on easy-to-follow ways for educators to eliminate such hazards, to broaden the spectrum of school-home interaction and to clean up the school's communication network.

SUGGESTED COMMUNICATION COMPONENTS
(School ——————— Home)

- Conduct town meetings on general policy and specific discipline problems in the school.
- Vary the time of open houses, PTSA meetings, student fairs, etc. (schedule some for afternoons or on weekends).
- Institute a program of home visitations utilizing administrators, teachers, paraprofessionals, etc. (If parents won't come to the school, the school *must* go to them.)
- Distribute a parent newsletter regularly—every principal should disseminate a personalized newsletter on a monthly or quarterly basis (see Sample Principal's Newsletter).
- Schedule occasional parent and community meetings away from the school.
- Establish a school "welcome wagon" program for new residents with school age and preschool children. (Volunteers, PTSA representatives, retired teachers, etc., may be used to implement such a program.)
- Schedule parent-teacher conferences at the secondary as well as the elementary level.
- Sponsor family wellness incentive programs.
- Open the school library to parent and public use.
- Use school CB radios to highlight accomplishments, advertise activities, and alert the community to problems areas.
- Conduct vandalism tours to show parents firsthand property defaced by students.
- Provide "You are Here" maps whenever parents enter the school.
- Convert an old school bus into a school mobile that can carry school news (e.g., curriculum outlines, new materials, samples of student work, achievement scores, attendance

Sample Principal's Newsletter

PRINCIPALLY SPEAKING

SCHOOL
LOGO

October, 1979

SCHOOL
ATMOSPHERE

I believe we have had one of the best school openings this
year in the history of St. Louis Park High School. The
attitude of the students has been excellent. I have been
impressed by the courtesy and cooperation demonstrated by
your sons and daughters. The mood of the school and
expressions from staff have been very positive. Please
extend my personal impressions to your students.

One of the major significant changes has occurred in student
program changes. Assistant Principal, Ade Leonhardi, and
the counselors took care of a majority of program change
requests before the school year began. This has enabled
students to be in classes of their choice with the first
day of school.

By not allowing smoking to take place in the building, the
loitering and attendant problems of littering and vandalism
have been markedly reduced. By re-instituting bells,
designating the start and end of class periods, the same
positive results have occurred.

STUDENTS
DRIVING
TO SCHOOL

Last May I encouraged parents to discourage students from
driving to school. The reasons stated were the energy
problems, increased gasoline prices and the limited number
of parking spaces. I am pleased to tell you that fewer
students are driving because the student parking areas now
have open spaces. Rather than school personnel prohibiting
students from driving to school, as some parents have
suggested, I would like to ask parents to control the
access to the car keys.

During the school day, 7:40 A.M. to 2:30 P.M., all thermostats
will be set at 65°. Parents and students should be advised
that during the upcoming cold weather season warm clothing
should be worn in school.

FUTURE
NEWSLETTERS

I am interested in including items of interest or concern to
you in future newsletters. If there is any special topic
you wish to have covered in an upcoming issue, please call me
at 925-4300, Ext. 125.

figures, photographs of property damage) into the neighborhoods of the community.

- Brag about your *nonproblems*. Publicize the percentage of students who have *not* been involved in vandalism, suspension, drug problems, truancy, etc. (Be your own best fan!)

- Use five-minute radio spots to feature school success stories and areas where help and support are needed.

- Report test scores and program evaluation results to parent groups *at the building level*. (Discuss "how our students are doing.")

- Devise ways to direct special attention to the parents of students who receive low citizenship marks.

- Plan a "Hands-on Nite" where parents can handle manipulative learning materials, micro-computers, etc.

- Hold selected school board meetings in neighborhood schools on a systematic rotating basis.

- Prepare and make available "Home Learning Recipes" for low-cost learning activities that parents can use at home.

- Use the community cablevision's educational and public access channels to air popular school programs and make important announcements.

- Involve parents and staff members in role playing exercises, value clarification demonstrations, and simulation games that clarify similarities and differences between the various role groups in the school.

- Provide taped messages on current school news and events.

- Video tape classes, assembly programs and student activities for showing to parent and civic groups.

- Encourage staff members to make frequent use of "Happy Grams" or "Good News Notes" (see Sample Good News Note Forms).

- Survey parent opinion on important school issues and use the results for concrete, visible improvement.

- Hold public hearings on every important change planned for the school.

- Use conference calls involving the principal, the teacher(s), and the parent(s) to reach decisions on pressing discipline problems.

(Sample Good News Note Form #1)

(Designed by Opal Oleson, art specialist and Nancy Kracke, Coordinator of Communication, for use in the St. Louis Park, MN. Public Schools)

(Sample Good News Note Form #2)

(Designed by Opal Oleson, art specialist and Nancy Kracke, Communications Coordinator, for use in the St. Louis Park, MN. Public Schools)

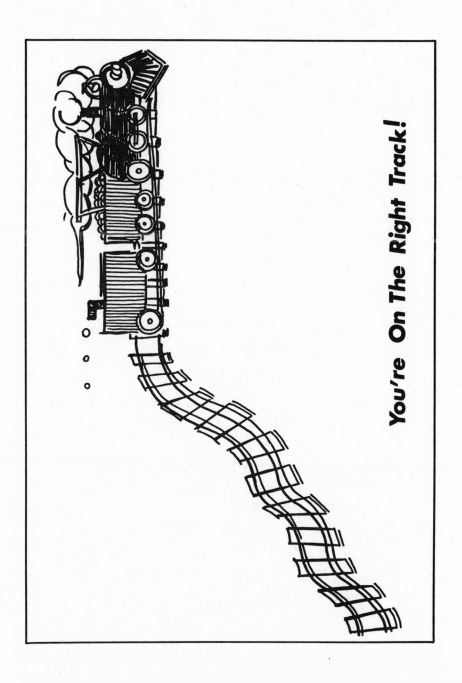

- Set aside the early portion of each school board and PTSA meeting for parent concerns and/or some good-news openers.

- Establish a safety hotline for use by parents.

- Conduct consumer evaluations of teachers, principals, and school board members performances. Publicize the results with specific betterment plans (see Sample Consumer Evaluation Survey Form).

- Implement a Positive Image Program (PIP) whereby every teacher or grade level holds an informal (but structured) meeting at least once each semester for all parents, to discuss key issues such as homework, discipline, grading philosophy, communication, transition to the next grade level, etc. The intent of these sessions should be to provide casual, intimate opportunity for parents to learn about the educational program, to get some of the questions answered that they have perhaps never asked, and to reach out and draw in some of those individuals who, for a variety of reasons, may not feel very close to their childrens' school.

SAMPLE CONSUMER EVALUATION SURVEY FORM

Cedarcrest Elementary School Parent Survey
Shakopee, MN

Please indicate your reaction to each of the following statements by circling the response that best describes how you feel.

Communications (Agree, Disagree, No Opinion)

1. There is a friendly attitude between parents and school staff.   A   D   N

2. The Cedarcrest newsletters provide good communication from the school to parents.   A   D   N

3. The school should continue to send community information (such as BAA, adult evening classes, etc.), home with children.   A   D   N

4. I am satisfied with the method of sending home notices of school activities with my child.   A   D   N

5. The Cedarcrest School handbook is valuable to use.   A   D   N

6. I feel free to communicate with all school personnel at Cedarcrest when necessary.   A   D   N

Special Services

1. The tutoring program has helped my child.   A   D   N

2. The speech therapy program at Cedarcrest has enabled my child with speech difficulties to learn and apply proper speech formations.   A   D   N

3. Title I language and math programs have benefited my child.   A   D   N

4. The Project Read program has helped my child with special reading difficulties in learning to read.   A   D   N

5. The learning center has helped my child with special learning needs.   A   D   N

6. The school psychologist has been helpful in testing and suggesting courses of action for children with special difficulties.   A   D   N

7. The school social worker has been helpful in aiding children to adjust better to the school situation.   A   D   N

8. The special music program (i.e., strings, band and chorus) in grades 5 and 6 gives the child a basic background in music.   A   D   N

Support Services

1. The resource center program provides a variety of materials and activities to enrich education for children.   A   D   N

2. CORA provides additional help for children in grades K-5.   A   D   N

3. School health programs (vision/hearing and nursing services) are adequate.　　A　D　N

4. I am satisfied with the atmosphere of the lunchroom.　　A　D　N

5. I am satisfied with current transportation procedures.　　A　D　N

6. The school food program offers nutritious and well-balanced meals.　　A　D　N

7. The school's safety patrol program is working well.　　A　D　N

8. Children in grades K-6 are attaining full potential in physical skills and muscle coordination in the phys ed program.　　A　D　N

Discipline

1. Discipline is fair and uniform for my child.　　A　D　N

2. The rights of my child are considered carefully in disciplinary actions.　　A　D　N

3. Discipline is administered in a manner making it a learning experience rather than a punishment.　　A　D　N

4. Classroom atmosphere provides an opportunity for maximum learning.　　A　D　N

5. Parents are consulted and involved in severe or repeated disciplinary situations.　　A　D　N

General School Climate

1. My child looks forward to going to school each day.　　A　D　N

2. Cedarcrest School has a positive effect on my child's general morale.　　A　D　N

3. The staff at Cedarcrest School shows concern for my child as an individual.　　A　D　N

4. Parents are encouraged to partici-
   pate as volunteers in various ways.   A   D   N

5. Parents are encouraged to visit their
   children's classroom during school
   hours.   A   D   N

6. Parents are encouraged to participate in PTA.   A   D   N

7. I am satisfied with Cedarcrest Elementary School.   A   D   N

Plant Facilities

1. The custodians keep Cedarcrest
   School neat and clean.   A   D   N

2. Cedarcrest School provides adequate comforts for children in the
   following areas:

      a. Restrooms   A   D   N

      b. Room temperature   A   D   N

      c. Classroom furniture   A   D   N

      d. Lighting   A   D   N

      e. Space for personal and
        school belongings   A   D   N

Curriculum (Too Much, Adequate, Too Little, No Opinion)

1. My child's needs are being met in
   each of the following areas:

      a. Reading   TM   A   TL   N

      b. Spelling   TM   A   TL   N

      c. Language/Grammar   TM   A   TL   N

      d. Mathematics   TM   A   TL   N

      e. Science   TM   A   TL   N

      f. Social Studies   TM   A   TL   N

      g. Physical Education   TM   A   TL   N

      h. Health   TM   A   TL   N

      i. Music   TM   A   TL   N

      j. Art   TM   A   TL   N

2. My child also is learning how to:

      a. Gain self-esteem/
        confidence   TM   A   TL   N

b. Develop self-discipline	TM	A	TL	N
c. Respect oneself and others	TM	A	TL	N
d. Be independent	TM	A	TL	N
e. Listen	TM	A	TL	N
f. Communicate	TM	A	TL	N
g. Share	TM	A	TL	N
h. Develop good work habits	TM	A	TL	N
i. Compete	TM	A	TL	N
j. Win/lose	TM	A	TL	N

If followed conscientiously, the kinds of communication practices described above can substantially strengthen the linkage between the home and the school and help shape an effective Parent Team approach to positive discipline.

One negative force that can rapidly erode school/home cooperation and distort effective communications is the presence of damaging rumors within the school community. The next portion of this chapter identifies some lasting ways to counteract the undermining effects of false rumors and inaccurate information about the school.

WAYS TO MAINTAIN
EFFECTIVE RUMOR CONTROL

Few single elements can jeopardize school communications and discipline efforts more completely than an unchallenged half-truth or untruth. False reports about conditions in the school or distorted news of efforts to control a situation can be devastating to any cooperative problem solving or discipline enforcement.

As insurance against rumor damage, it is essential that school personnel design some effective means of detecting falsehoods in their pre-emergent stage and of setting the record straight when full-blown mistruths surface in the community. The school must have a ready-made vehicle for getting the facts out fast in times of crisis. Traditional communication channels are often too slow to head off a "mess in the making."

Many schools attempt to limit and/or defuse the spread of rumors by adopting one or more of the following stop-gap precautions:

1. Issuing rumor sheets followed by fact sheets as quickly as possible. These are often distributed by sending them home with students to bypass any delays in mailing.

2. Extending an open invitation for all interested parties to come to the school to see for themselves what conditions are really like and whether or not rumor reports are true.

3. Establishing hot lines with recorded messages designed to dispel doubts and provide factual information.

Although these techniques are helpful, a more far-reaching and permanent approach to maintaining effective rumor control is to develop a network of *key communicators* throughout the community who can be contacted quickly when needed. This concept, which has been endorsed by the National School Public Relations Association (NSPRA) and a variety of other professional organizations, is explained in detail in the following paragraphs.

The purpose of a key communications program is to set in place an authorized grapevine through which school authorities can be alerted to rumblings and rumors as early as possible and by which factual information can be disseminated throughout the community quickly and reliably. The persons who comprise this network must be respected as well as generally knowledgeable and aware of school and community affairs.

The cadre of key communicators should be made up of citizens who are visible, available, and credible. They should reflect a cross section of the population and each should have many contacts in several segments of the community. Such networks typically include a variety of occupations and professions such as journalists, doctors, bartenders, political figures, labor leaders, senior citizens, hair stylists, housewives, secretaries, ministers, etc.

To make the network operational, it is important that school authorities share information (e.g., program proposals, long-range plans, meeting agendas, budget materials, background documents, etc.), on a regular basis. It is also often advisable to develop such a network at both the building and the district level.

The first step in organizing a key communications program is to identify prospective participants who talk to and are listened to by a wide circle of community members. A simple technique for making this identification is to conduct a low-key Community Leadership Analysis. In this approach, positional leaders in the community (e.g., office holders, civic club officers, elected officials, etc.) and long-time residents are asked to nominate five people whom they believe to be most knowledgeable and informed regarding school and civic affairs. (See sample Community Leadership Analysis Letter.)

SAMPLE COMMUNITY LEADERSHIP ANALYSIS LETTER

Dear_____:

One of the goals of our schools is to identify respected key communicators in our district who can assist us in providing more and better information to the total public. To accomplish this, we are contacting persons, like yourself, who hold leadership positions and/or who have been long-time residents of the community, for assistance.

Would you please take a few minutes to list below the five people whom you feel are most knowledgeable and informed of community and school affairs:

Nominations for
Community Leadership Analysis

Name   *Address* (if possible)

1.
2.
3.
4.
5.

Please return your nominations in the self-enclosed envelope by _____19_____. If you have any questions about this survey, please feel free to contact me. Thank you for your help.

Appreciatively,

Once the first nominations are received, a list is developed of individuals who received one or more nominations and whose names were not included on the initial mailing list. These persons are then sent a similar letter soliciting their nominations.

After the two-cycle survey is completed, the responses are tallied and ranked in order of nomination frequency. The citizens at the top of this rank-order listing make up potential key communicators.

The next step is to explain the program to potential participants and to elicit their involvement. This may be done at a brief organizational meeting or through a letter of invitation. (See Sample Key Communicators Letter of Invitation below.)

SAMPLE KEY COMMUNICATORS LETTER OF INVITATION

Dear _____:

This is a letter to ask you to serve on an important school committee. But wait! Before you groan "Oh no! Not another committee!", please read on.

This committee has no officers. It presents no reports to the Board. In fact, it never meets. All the members have to do is pick up their mail.

We are asking you to become part of a school information network. We will send to you copies of important reports received by the School Board, summaries of Board meetings in the internal District Staffletter, copies of brochures, budget development figures, and other information we think you should know.

What's your part in this network? We just want you to read the materials sent to you. No reports—no speeches to civic groups. Just read.

And then when you are at a meeting or a party or just visiting across the fence, and the subject of schools comes up, would you do this for us: would you use your knowledge of our schools to set the record straight, to clear up misconceptions, to add perspective to the conversation?

That's all.

We would like you to be a member of our information network because people listen to you. You are a credible person in the community and a supporter of education. You know that support of public education is based on an informed citizenry. We will continue to inform residents through established programs and publications. But since we can't be present at the backyard visits and the neighborhood get-togethers, we hope you might fill in for us.

We will begin sending information to you on _____, 19____. If you would *not* like to participate in the information network, please let me know by

_____, 19_____ and I will see that your name is
taken off our mailing list.
    If you have questions please call me. Thank you!
Sincerely,

Once established, a key communicators network can function almost automatically and can play a powerful role in deflating rumors and assisting the school to maintain a cooperative base of support for its educational and discipline programs.

In addition to strengthening communications and constraining the spread of rumors, one of the most simple and direct approaches to forming a constructive partnership with parents is the effective use of parent advisory committees. On the other hand, ill-conceived and mismanaged advisory groups can do irreparable harm to the Parent Team concept. The following section contains some simple, sensible directions for assuring that such committees are positive and productive.

WORKABLE PARENT ADVISORY COMMITTEES

If properly directed, fully functioning parent advisory committees can be a forceful ally of the school staff in dealing with a variety of discipline problems. Experience across the nation reflects considerable variation in the purpose, makeup and function of such groups. Examples include School Climate Committees, Security Advisory Committees, Bus Behavior Committees, etc. One guiding principle that is applicable to all school advisory bodies is that they should deal with general policy and not with specific practices and procedures (e.g., it is appropriate for a citizens committee to assist in the development of an overall truancy policy, but it is not advisable for such a group to meet on each and every truancy case).

The most commonly accepted legitimate functions of an outside advisory group include the following:

a. questioning/inquiring

b. examining/studying

c. gathering data/research

d. synthesizing

e. identifying problem areas

f. informing

g. suggesting/recommending

h. evaluating

i. reporting results

The conditions and considerations necessary to provide the proper framework for a fully functioning advisory committee are itemized below:

Step 1   Define the degree of influence and the area(s) of responsibility. (There must be a common understanding of the meaning of the term, *advisory*.)

Step 2   Limit the focus. (Define the charge.)

Step 3   Ascertain whether the committee is to be ad hoc or continuing. (For most purposes, ad hoc committees work best.)

Step 4   Determine membership parameters (e.g., proportion of parents, teachers, administrators, students, etc.; length of term; staggering of initial terms; and selection procedures).

Step 5   Identify leadership.

Step 6   Establish operating rules.

Step 7   Provide appropriate background information.

Step 8   Make provision for adequate record keeping and reporting.

Step 9   Set target date for completion.

Step 10 Provide resources and help as needed.

Step 11 Get out of the way!

In addition to adhering to the structure outlined above, the best way to assure positive advisory committee outcomes is to avoid the following stumbling blocks that are identified below.

Ten Obstacles to Effective
Advisory Committee Operations

- Ill-defined problem/need—no real purpose for the committee.

- Membership that is not representative. (If staff members are included, they should always constitute a clear-cut minority on the committee.)
- Too large a membership.
- Bad timing (established prematurely or too close to the end of the school year).
- Lack of resources (e.g., funds, clerical assistance) for committee work.
- Information overkill (providing too much too soon).
- The intrusion of politics.
- No provision for evaluation.
- Committee recommendations that provide no alternatives for the school board or the school staff.
- Lack of specific action on committee recommendations and/or lack of recognition for committee work.

The two sample policies that follow provide further illustrations of sound approaches to utilizing advisory committees to the best advantage.

(Sample Policy)

DISTRICT SENIOR HIGH SCHOOL COMMUNICATIONS COMMITTEE
(Cedar Rapids, IA, Community Schools)

A district Senior High School Communications Committee shall be established whose purpose shall be to broaden the scope of communication among and between students, teachers, parents, and the administrative staff, and to advise the administration regarding matters of concerns to students. The Executive Director-Secondary Education shall schedule meetings of the committee and prepare the agenda for each meeting. At least five meetings shall be held each year.

Each senior high school shall be represented by one parent, one teacher, one administrator, and three students. Procedures that ensure democratic representation of students and parents shall be established by each high school. If minorities are not otherwise represented on the committee, the school with the greatest minority population shall select an additional member who shall be a minority student. If the Board wishes to be represented on the committee, a Board member may be appointed to serve as an additional adult member.

Annually, the committee shall prepare and submit a report that contains an assessment of the effectiveness of its work. When appropriate, recommendations concerning improvement of committee procedure and/or the communications process shall be included in the report. The report shall be submitted to the Executive Director-Secondary Education at the end of each school year.

(Sample Policy)

Westwood Community Schools
(Omaha, NB)

Advisory Groups or Committees for the Board

The Board may appoint advisory committees to study problems and recommend solutions, provide information, or perform assigned tasks as directed by the Board of Education and administered by the Superintendent.

The members of each group shall be instructed regarding the length of time each is being asked to serve, and the service the Board wishes it to render. Furthermore, the group shall be instructed regarding its relationship with the Board and with the staff.

The Board shall have sole power to dissolve any of its advisory groups at any time during the life of the group.

Structure and Composition

The Board shall adopt whatever advisory group structure and organization it deems appropriate to the assignment at hand. The type of Board-appointed group shall be as follows:

1. The size and composition of the group shall be determined by the Board according to the group function.

2. There shall be a beginning date, purpose, and ending date.

3. If staff members are appointed to any citizens' advisory committee for the Board, they shall constitute a minority of any such committee.

Joint Meetings

If the group is a committee and the assigned function necessitates a meeting with the Board, such a joint meeting should be arranged by the Superintendent.

Minutes of the joint meeting will be recorded and copies of the minutes will be submitted to the Board and committee members.

Correspondence

Correspondence between the Board and its advisory group will be coordinated by the Superintendent.

As indicated earlier, the successful management of parent advisory committees can be a powerful asset and adjunct to the school's discipline program. Nevertheless, the success of a Parent Team approach cannot rely on advisory groups alone.

Another component of the school's partnership with the home that is becoming increasingly important and has direct bearing on school discipline now and in the future is the emergence of *parenting education* programs. The final part of this chapter is devoted to detailing some new, nontheoretical ideas for implementing a successful program in this area.

DEVELOPING A SUCCESSFUL
PARENTING EDUCATION PROGRAM

If the school can play a significant role in improving parenting practices, all parties in the learning community, (e.g., parents, students, and school personnel) benefit immeasurably. In simple terms, better training may mean better parents, better homes, better prepared pupils, and consequently, better discipline in the school.

For these reasons, some form of parenting education is rapidly becoming a vital catalyst in the chemistry of a Parent Team approach to problem solving in many districts. From the school's perspective, the payoffs of a sound parenting program are both immediate and long range. Parenting education strengthens the discipline skills of parents, reinforces the home-school relationship, and partially answers the school's obligation to address total community needs.

One success secret of an effective program is to introduce training early and to repeat opportunities at various levels so that parents can enter or re-enter at different points in time in accordance with their needs. Many school systems now offer parenting education as part of the regular curriculum for secondary students, in prenatal classes for expectant parents, to parents of preschool children, and as an ongoing program available to all parents of school-age children and youth. Such offerings are commonly provided through the district's adult or community education services. These programs may range from loosely knit parent support groups meeting on a regular basis with a facilitator-leader in sessions where no final answers are expected, to highly structured formal courses of instruction.

Where young parents are involved, it is essential that babysitting services be provided in conjunction with the parent classes. For purposes of illustration, a sampling of the kinds of topics frequently covered in a short course for parents of preschool children is included below.

Parenting of Preschool Children—
Sample Topics

1. Building your child's confidence and feelings of self-worth
2. How children think—seminar on children's thought processes
3. Children's sexuality
4. Encouragement
5. CPR
6. Drug awareness
7. Changing children's misbehavior
8. TV viewing—Its effect on your child
9. What to do when "everybody's doing it"
10. Alternatives in discipline
11. Introduction to behavior modification

---

12. Handling childhood fears
13. What research says about parenting
14. Tell me another story, daddy!
       and another
          and another
             and another

Wherever possible, effort should be made to fit the parenting program to unique community characteristics and needs (e.g., incidence of single-parent families, parenting patterns among different ethnic groups represented in the population, etc.). For this purpose, a well-balanced advisory committee can be invaluable in designing a tailor-made comprehensive program.

Typically, the makeup of such advisory boards includes representatives of the following community groups:

a. Parents (a special effort should be made to involve fathers)

b. Teachers (especially early childhood education specialists)

c. Health agencies

d. Social agencies

e. Legislators

f. Clergy

g. Legal advisors

h. Counselors

Where appropriate, a well-rounded parenting education program should incorporate separate components aimed at the needs of special parent groups such as:

- Adoptive parents
- Parents of twins
- Second family parents
- Expectant parents
- Parents of infants
- Teen parents
- Handicapped parents
- Foreign speaking parents
- Parents of chronically ill children

- Dads' discussion groups
- Later life parents
- Single parents (see sample format below)

Sample Format
for
Single Parent Class

5:30-6:00 p.m.—Potluck supper
6:00-6:30 p.m.—Parent/child playtime
6:30-7:30 p.m.—Parent discussion group (child care
                        provided)

Most current programs are built around a *philosophy of parenting* that features the following common tenets:

1. Every person (regardless of age) has worth and should be accorded equal respect and dignity.
2. Every individual should have the freedom to be him or herself.
3. Parenting is a difficult art for which there is minimal preparation or assistance.
4. Parents are certain to make mistakes, but they can recover and learn from their errors.
5. Every person has the right to attempt to fill his/her own needs.
6. Conversely, no person has the right to do damage to another while filling his/her own needs.
7. Parents have an obligation to facilitate the child's quest for independence.
8. No parent-child relationship is trouble free.
9. Parents need their own time, space, and privacy just as children do.
10. There is no single right way to be a parent.

A suggested framework for approaching basic parenting education is contained in the sample course outline.

PYRAMID FOR PARENT INVOLVEMENT

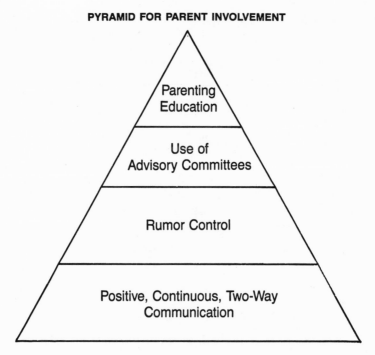

Figure 7-2

(Sample Course Outline)

THE ART OF PARENTING

(A parenting curriculum developed by the pupil services department of the St. Louis Park, Minnesota Public Schools)

*Basic Units

- "Didn't you hear what I said?" (communication)
- "Can't I have a little peace and quiet around here?" (order and routine)
- "Who is in charge here, anyway?" (independence and responsibility)
- "Just who do you think you are?" (identity)
- "You could do better if you'd only try." (competition)
- "I've just about had it!" (parental needs)

> *Each unit is divided into sections on problem definition, possible approaches, skill development, and evaluation and task challenges.

The ideas and examples outlined in this chapter provide down-to-earth examples for integrating parenting educations into the school's Parent Team approach to positive discipline.

All of the previous sections illustrate effective ways that school authorities can harness parent power to help establish a positive and peaceful educational climate. Together these strategies constitute a total package for developing the Parent Team concept as illustrated in the Pyramid for Parent Involvement.

Without parent cooperation and support, the school's efforts to maintain reasoned and responsible behavior are doomed to failure. In terms of maintaining proper pupil conduct and control, there is special truth in the ancient Chinese proverb that proclaims, "One parent is worth a thousand teachers." For school officials concerned about discipline, reaching the family is as important as reaching the child. The final prerequisite for securing parental cooperation is that teachers and principals most consistently be "up front" about all discipline matters and problems.

Based on the kind of positive parent support explained above, Chapter 8 presents a practical bazaar of classroom-proven action plans and alternative programs that have helped schools to overcome serious discipline problems and restore harmonious pupil-teacher, pupil-pupil relationships.

8

Developing Positive Programs for Negative Students

The more successful and satisfying the learning environment is for every pupil, the fewer the number of discipline problems that will arise. In discipline matters, as in sports, the best defense is often a good offense. The "smart school" is assertive, affirmative, and proactive in going on the offensive to avert problems by providing positive programs for all students. The goal is to ensure a rich mixture of experiences and opportunities through the creative use of all available resources.

Every child deserves to find a comfortable, rewarding niche in school—some program that provides real challenge and genuine gratification. For some, this niche may be a part of the regular curriculum or an appropriate alternative program during the normal school day. For others, it may be in some extension or supplement to the standard program outside regular school hours. This chapter presents a straightforward discussion of children-tested programs that can turn on turned-off students and improve school discipline.

IMPROVING OUTLETS FOR ENERGY— AN EFFECTIVE ACTIVITY PROGRAM

Many schools find that one significant way to reduce unrest and prevent discipline problems is to broaden participation and energize the school's program of extracurricular and co-curricular activities. A successful activity program can be introduced at any elementary or secondary level.

Contrary to the thinking of some educational purists, the school's activity program is not merely the frosting on the cake— rather, it is an essential part of the texture of the school. For some students it is the only thing that makes sense in the school!

The benefits of a sound, comprehensive activity program are many and varied, including the following:

- Fosters personal-social development
- Teaches new skills, knowledge, and attitudes
- Intensifies student involvement
- Builds confidence and self-esteem
- Adds excitement
- Humanizes the school
- Breaks up cliques
- Enhances staff involvement
- Affords an opportunity to present staff in different role
- Provides practice and application of skills learned in the regular program
- Builds spirit/morale
- Provides diversion
- Expands parent interest and involvement
- Serves as an energy outlet
- Extends the curriculum
- Improves public relations

But, perhaps the greatest benefit is simply better behavior and feelings in the school.

In order to reap these benefits, the criteria noted below may assist school staffs in putting together a well-rounded package of extracurricular and co-curricular experiences and opportunities.

**EARMARKS OF AN EFFECTIVE
ACTIVITIES PROGRAM**

_____ Is fluid to fit the ebb and flow of student interests, needs, and priorities.

_____ Involves real *learning*.

_____ Is accessible and affordable.

_____ Is democratic and nondiscriminatory.

_____ Stresses cooperation as well as competition.

_____ Includes equal opportunities for both sexes.

_____ Eliminates elitism and strives to tap the uninvolved.

_____ Maximizes participation.

_____ Recognizes and fosters ethnic pride and awareness.

_____ Provides adapted opportunities and activities for the handicapped.

_____ Features qualified and interested advisors, coaches, and other adult leaders.

_____ Uses community resources.

_____ Opens up leadership opportunities to members of all student groups.

_____ Provides rewards and _recognition_.

As indicated by the checklist above, the successful activity program is not limited to a few select areas of excellence; rather, it reflects variety and balance. Of course, it is possible for a school or district to offer too much or too little in terms of activities. Prudence must prevail. But whatever is offered should be designed to suit the audience(s) and to offer _something_ for everyone, as depicted in the Activities Grid (Figure 8-1).

ACTIVITIES GRID

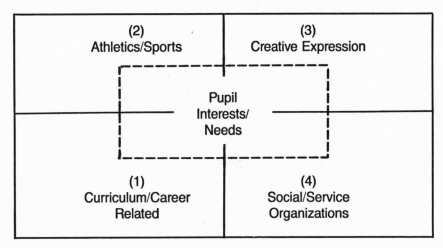

Figure 8-1

Quadrant 1—Represents curriculum enrichment programs and organizations (e.g., math club, science club, etc.), and the variety of career exploration groups that can be offered under school auspices.

Quadrant 2—Includes all of the interscholastic, intramural, and individual athletics and sports programs provided by the school. (May encompass fitness and conditioning programs as well.)

Quadrant 3—Involves all of the extracurricular opportunities for artistic expression sponsored by the school.

Quadrant 4—May include a wide spectrum of groups organized to provide service to the school or community and/ or to promote a well-rounded social life in the school.

Pupil Interests/ Needs— The area of pupil concerns, needs, and interests is the one element that touches all of the other activity quadrants, providing the only legitimate reasons for their existence. The entire activity program must focus on and be structured around this segment.

The kind of desired diverse and balanced activity program represented in the Activities Grid is further illustrated by the Partial List of Sample Activities that follows. Few schools will offer all of these programs, but every school should provide at least a minimum sampling of opportunities from each category.

Although the rudiments of a dynamic and defensible activity program are suggested in the activities' list, no array of activities will have a positive impact on discipline if the students don't participate. The extent of student involvement in activities is one of the real clues to the climate in any school.

The history of public education in this country clearly reveals that a phenomenon of *causative reciprocity* (an inverse cause and effect relationship) exists between participation in school activities and discipline problems. The lower the involvement, the higher the incidence of disruption and vice versa. This was most recently demonstrated during the Viet Nam era when student participation dipped to an extremely low level and the incidence of protests in schools rose to new heights. Thus, it behooves the school staff to encourage involvement and to stimulate the student activity

Curric./Career Related	Athletics/Sports	Creative Expression	Social/Service Organizations
Debate	Football	Madrigals	Jr. Red Cross
Journalism	Basketball	Jazz Ensemble	Key Club
Student Government	Baseball	Rock Groups	Safety Patrol
High School Bowl	Track	Art Exhibits	Ecology Club
Social Sci. Sem.	Cross Country Track	Forensics	Pep Club
Model UN	Hockey	Dance Troupes	Welcome Committee
Foreign Lang. Club	Soccer	Folk Music Groups	Ham Radio Club
Future Farmers	Swimming	Literary Magazines	Candy Stripers
Jr. Achievement	Wrestling	Dance/Stage Band	Pen Pals
Science Club	Gymnastics	Quill and Scroll	Civil Air Patrol
Industrial Arts Fairs	Synchronized Swimming	Summer Stock	Peer Tutoring
Future Teachers	Skiing (slalom)	Talent Shows	Civic Volunteers
Art Club	Skiing (cross county)	Youth Opera	Prom Committee
National Honor Society	Golf	One Act Plays	PTSA
Future Business Leaders	Tennis	Musicals	Consumer Groups
4-H	Softball	Square Dance	Campaign Workers
Math Club	Water Polo	Three Act Plays	Letter Winners Club
Future Homemakers	Rowing	Declamation Contests	Charities
Rocketry	Boxing	Thespians	Cultural Exchange
Psychology Club	Table Tennis	Drill Team	Ushers/Usherettes
Livestock Judging	Bowling	Barber Shop Quartet	Water Safety Club
Mock Legislature	Roller Skating	Crafts Fairs	Am. Field Service
Medical Careers Club	Rugby	Camera Club	Teen Appreciation Club

program where necessary. A few simple ways for maximizing participation are identified below.

Ways to Improve Participation

1. Publicize widely the times and locations of all tryouts, auditions, informational meetings, etc.

2. Conduct student interest surveys and use the results to shape future programming.

3. Increase the size of teams, casts, music groups, etc.

4. Have an Activities Fair for students and parents.

5. Include as many dates of activities as possible in the official school calendar and distribute widely.

6. Strive for convenient scheduling. Vary the times of activities. Schedule some before school, some during the school day when feasible, some immediately after school, some in the evenings, and some on weekends.

7. Practice creative recruiting. Use personal contacts. Encourage team captains, club presidents, and other student leaders to be ambassadors for recruiting.

8. Adopt a no-cut policy.

9. Consider *all* religious holidays in scheduling activities.

10. Use homerooms to promote and explain activities.

11. Consider an activity period during the school day (particularly at the middle school and junior high school level).

12. Provide transportation where possible (e.g., an activity bus run to accommodate students who remain after the regular school day to participate in activities).

13. Stress the benefits of the activity program at orientation meetings for students and parents.

14. Minimize conditions/prerequisites for participation (e.g., scholastic requirements).

15. Promote parent/community booster clubs.

16. Encourage counselors to provide guidance in activity selection as well as course selection.

17. Distribute a Guide to Student Activities along with the regular registration guide of courses at enrollment time.

18. Conduct special meetings for the parents of students involved in different activities (e.g., basketball parents; band parents, etc.).

19. Highlight students who achieve in activities (e.g., Student of the Week).

20. Use alumni and local celebrities to discuss with students what activities have contributed to their lives.

21. Beef up the awards program. Invest in quality letters, plaques, certificates, etc. (Include all areas, not just athletics.)

The final watchword for managing and maintaining a lively and popular activity program is to exert every effort to *make it easy* for students *to start* participating and *worthwhile* for them *to continue.*

Although a vital co-curricular activity program is a must for maximizing student involvement, it is still within the instructional program during the regular school day that the staff must find ways to keep students attending, learning, and at peace with and in the school. For certain students, this requires creative and sometimes unorthodox education programming.

The next section profiles a collection of programs in representative school systems that have demonstrated success in reducing dropouts and improving behavior in the school.

EXAMPLES OF SUCCESSFUL DROPOUT PREVENTION PROGRAMS

Many effective school districts have initiated special programs to prevent dropouts and redirect disruptive students. Based on the experience of many of these systems, the following conditions seem essential to the favorable implementation of an alternative dropout prevention program:

A. Teachers who are truly interested in working with discipline problems. (Because of the emotional overload involved in this type of teaching, burnout often occurs within three to five years.)

B. Tangible support (e.g., class size, space, materials) and funding. Survival of special dropout programs is more likely if the programs can be largely locally funded and entail no significant increases in per pupil costs.

C. Flexibility that allows nontraditional content and process.

D. A well-conceived plan for identification, screening, and assignment.

E. A curriculum that is perceived by students to be immediately relevant and practical.

F. Parental and administrative support.

G. Community input.

To avoid hit or miss programming, some educators find it helpful to have an established policy to guide the orderly development of alternative or atypical approaches. The sample below offers one model for such a policy statement.

(Sample Policy)

ALTERNATIVE EDUCATION PROGRAMS

(Wichita, KS, Public Schools)

The Wichita Public Schools shall provide alternative education programs to meet the needs of individuals at preschool, elementary, secondary, post secondary, and adult education levels. These are all full-service programs that meet the objectives and requirements of a conventional program of the same developmental level. Enrollment in these programs is available on an open and/or voluntary basis. Alternative programs may be housed in the conventional school or in shared facilities. A building principal may provide alternative programs within an existing authorized school program. The total educational offering for an individual school may be an alternative education program, with the general support of the community and the approval of the Board of Education.

The remainder of this section examines a representative sampling of school districts that have pioneered successful dropout prevention programs that have improved both attendance (retention) and discipline.

Seattle WA. Public Schools

(JALE)—Joyful Alternative Learning Experience

This dropout-oriented program stresses work experience, community relations, and basic-skills development. Each student participates in a diagnostic interview that leads to a contract prescribing the work/experiences necessary to satisfy the program's objectives. A major effort is made to foster a responsible attitude toward the community and students frequently become involved in community improvement projects.

Interim School

This alternative provides a flexible program for students who are not actively involved in any other regular or alternative school program. On a contract basis, the pupils (including suspended students) earn diploma credit. Students are generally enrolled in Interim on a short-term basis.

(P. S. #1)—People's School Number 1

P. S. #1 is designed for students who are dropouts or have been suspended from regular junior or senior high school. Goals include offering credit courses, providing job counseling and placement, and referring students and their families to appropriate social service agencies.

Project Interchange

This alternative junior-senior high program is for pupils whose grades, attitudes, and behavior indicate that they are on their way to dropping out of school. The program features highly individualized instruction and continuous progress concepts. A broadly based advisory committee serves to improve communication, identify resources, and maintain public support.

Roosevelt Tune-Inn

The Tune-Inn program offers individual attention, personally relevant classes, and the opportunity for small group discussion in a less-structured, off-campus environment. Tune-Inn provides a time away from the traditional program in which the students involved have ceased to learn. In its less-structured milieu, personal reflection (especially regarding future planning and educational goals) is encouraged.

Students attend classes each day. Mandatory individual classes are held twice weekly for 90-minute periods. One day each week is reserved for general school meetings. Special guests and field trips are scheduled on these days. Kitchen facilities are available. At least one overnight trip is included in the program.

Grand Rapids (MI) Public Schools

Juvenile Ombudsman

The juvenile ombudsman program attempts to address the needs of the community's juvenile delinquent population. Ombudsmen serve students referred by school or court personnel. The program is also available to any student in need of help to solve personal, family, or school problems.

Street Academy

This alternative secondary school serves students who are alienated from the regular school setting. The program, which is designed to be both rehabilitative and preventive, offers a wide range of subjects taught on an individual basis. Staff members also concentrate on helping students learn to exhibit socially acceptable behavior.

Come Back School

This alternative community education program focuses on poorly motivated teenage youths (many are juvenile offenders) who have dropped out, been dismissed from, or failed in all other school settings. The program is based on the belief that these students need to experience themselves "making it" in school; consequently, this specialized program assures success for each student by daily revision and prescription of the pupil's personal curriculum.

Sweet Street Academy

This alternative elementary school is aimed at students (grades 3-6) who are having difficulty experiencing success in school. The school features an individualized instructional program with emphasis on self-concept development. A strong emphasis is also placed on the reasons for studying the curriculum in an effort to achieve greater perceived relevancy.

New Orleans (LA) Public Schools

Five Alternative Schools

The New Orleans Public Schools have established five alternative schools designed to treat the causes of truancy and disruptive behavior. Enrollment is voluntary. Students sign a contract that commits them to try to change their behavior and setting a date by which improvement will be achieved. Parents also sign a contract agreeing to the following conditions:

- attend specified meetings/assemblies
- provide accurate daytime telephone numbers
- check with counselors regularly
- visit the school unannounced each six weeks
- assure that nightly homework assignments are completed

In addition to problem counseling and individual instruction in problem areas, the schools offer a regular curriculum, student government, and extracurricular activities.

Cedar Rapids (IA) Community Schools

Metro High School

This is a specialized school that offers a second chance to earn a diploma. Students must have been dropouts for at least 30 days and must be under 21 years of age. The program is built around several themes, including: basic skills, survival skills, career development, citizenship, and personal enrichment. The school operates with only three rules:

1. No drugs or alcohol on school property.
2. Leave pets and babies at home.
3. Be at school every day and be busy.

(O.A.K.)-Opportunities at Kirkwood

The O.A.K. program brings together the resources of the local community college and the public schools to help students who have dropped out to resume an education. O.A.K. opportunities include "packaged" courses in many areas, special interest classes (including classes offered by the community college throughout the city), counseling and career training programs.

Plymouth-Canton (MI) Community Schools

Student Service Center

The Student Service Center uses peers to provide support for students experiencing difficulty in the regular school environment and focuses on behaviors or unmet needs that inhibit success in the classroom. Services available include:

A. Individualized projects: Students withdrawn from classes for poor attendance may elect to earn credit through an individual project. Students must sign a contract and credit is granted only on the basis of successful completion of the objectives.

B. Tutoring and study skill development.

C. Crisis intervention.

D. Outreach.

E. Services to reentering students.

F. General school services.

Alternative 2

This program enables students who are withdrawn from school for falling below a three-class minimum, but who are successful in at least two classes, to continue to gain credit. Eligible students are technically withdrawn, but have the option of continuing to work from the classes in which they are succeeding during after school hours. Individual projects for credit are also available for some students (see Alternative 2 Referral Form below).

ALTERNATIVE 2 REFERRAL FORM

_____is being referred to the
          (student name)
Alternative 2 program. Records indicate that he/she has made satisfactory progress in _____ and _____.
                        (class)   (class)
     The student will meet with the coordinator of the Alternative 2 program to discuss that involvement on _____ at _____.
                             (time)

Area Coordinator	Teacher
Student	Teacher
Parent	Coordinator Alternative 2

Ultimate involvement will depend on the outcome of this meeting and the ability to coordinate assignments with the remaining teachers.

Growthworks Programs

Growthworks, Inc. (a locally based agency) uses its Youth Center to provide a natural setting for alienated students to become reinvolved in school. The program is designed for students who need some means of continuing their education while learning to accept responsibility and to be accountable for their behavior. Growthworks provides an approachable environment, close individual contact, and parental involvement.

Hastings, MN

FOCUS

This successful program for dealing with disaffected youth provides an alternative educational plan (school within a school) for students lacking in motivation, confidence, and self-esteem. The FOCUS program attempts to:

a. reduce student dissatisfaction with school and learning.

b. improve basic skills.

c. build a classroom culture that demonstrates the caring principle.

d. improve student ability to relate effectively with peers and adults.

e. give students a reason to be optimistic about the future.

All FOCUS students are involved in a group counseling experience called FAMILY. Each FAMILY consists of eight to ten students and one teacher who meet one hour each day.

All of the programs capsulized above typify the efforts that creative schools and school districts have undertaken to develop positive programs capable of reaching and teaching problem students and/or potential dropouts. In designing such special programs, it is important to keep in mind that the prospective clientele comprises a rich mixture of misfits, misdirected or unmotivated students, educationally disabled learners, and young people in pain. Students who represent dropouts-in-the-making and who may require special programming include all of the following:

1. The loners and the lonely
2. The troubled and trouble-prone (the delinquent)
3. The drug users
4. The "free spirits"
5. The students who must work
6. The emotionally immature
7. The students returning from treatment or correctional institutions
8. The victims of personal problems
9. The pregnant and/or married
10. The battered child

To be successful, a dropout prevention program must be responsive, sensitive, and flexible enough to accommodate the needs of each of these types of students and many others.

All of the programs described in this section, as well as scores of other successful projects throughout the country, share certain common strands that seem to characterize successful programs. Some of these traits are identified below:

Common Traits of Successful Dropout Prevention (Alternative) Programs

- Small groups
- Specific objectives
- Alternative curriculums
- Voluntary involvement (for both students and staff)
- Some form of "paced" courses
- Stress on socialization skills
- Emphasis on reading
- Work-study component
- Absence of overpermissiveness
- Parent contact

- Immediate student success
- Constant encouragement (reminder phone calls, etc.)
- Low profile (limited publicity)
- Careful evaluation
- Upfront dealing with drugs
- Personal goal setting
- Element of informality (e.g., first names, etc.)

In many situations, an alternative program or school-within-a-school that encompasses the characteristics above is an essential element in striving for control and student welfare. Such programs, however, should be only one part of the school's educational and discipline plan. They should not constitute the sole approach to providing positive programs for negative students.

The next section features a variety of other kinds of action plans that have proved to have a positive effect on borderline students and on discipline in general at both the elementary and secondary levels.

SAMPLE ACTION PLANS
FOR ELEMENTARY AND SECONDARY SCHOOLS

Beyond pumping additional adrenalin into the activity program and providing alternative dropout prevention programs, many schools have implemented other kinds of specific action plans aimed at improving behavior and enchancing order in the school.

The range of these "extra effort" programs encompasses a wide variety of approaches, including:

- setting up "cool off" rooms;
- introducing "moonrise" programs (offered after school hours for problem students excluded from day school, working students, "night people," etc.);
- providing management aides in the classroom;
- enrolling adults in high school courses;
- establishing "fundamental schools," etc.

In all cases, the intent is to focus special attention and resources on one or more specific problem areas through a carefully developed plan of action.

This section examines a cross section of such programs that have worked in a number of typical school districts.

One of the most popular recent discipline developments in many schools has been the inclusion of some form of in-house suspension for student offenders. Although formats vary, the general purpose of these programs is to provide a temporary period of supervised isolation, in order to help problem students while they "get their act together." A few examples of effective in-house suspension programs are cited below.

I.S.S. (In-School Suspension)

The Ozark City (AL) School System experienced a 40 percent drop in suspensions over a one year period following introduction of its In-School Suspension (I.S.S.) program. I.S.S. at Ozark City is designed to administer appropriate punishment to disruptive students, while at the same time, keeping these students under direct supervision by school authorities. A student's willingness to cooperate, as judged by the faculty supervisor, is the prerequisite for release after a prescribed period of I.S.S. suspension.

Room 11

At Grafton (MA) Senior High School, an in-school suspension procedure identified as *Room 11* has proved successful in reducing absenteeism and skipping teacher-assigned detention periods. Grafton students having continuing behavioral or serious discipline problems may be assigned to Room 11 for a class period, a day, or some other defined length of time. While in Room 11, students lose one point from the quarter grade of each class missed. Rules in Room 11 include "no talking" and "no privilege to leave."

Alternative Learning Program (ALP)

The purpose of the Alternative Learning Program at Sandburg Middle School (Anoka, MN) is to remove disruptive students from the regular instructional programs and to isolate them for a minimum of one school day. Students are placed in ALP only after other methods of discipline have proved unsuccessful. The students are constantly supervised by staff members throughout the day and given assignments to complete while they are in the program. Each teacher who is responsible for any part of the child's academic program is responsible for completing an assignment sheet on the morning(s) that the student is to be assigned to ALP.

The Cube

Rule breakers at Oak Creek (WI) Senior High sometimes find themselves isolated in a converted foreign language laboratory known as the *Cube*. In the Cube, all socializing is banned and students work in separated carrels. Students eat lunch at their desks and must be escorted to and from the lavatories.

Alternative Room

The suspension rate at Central Jr. High School (Lawrence, KS) fell from 1.8 students per day in 1974-75 to .4 students in 1978-79 following inauguration of an in-house suspension program called the *Alternative Room*. The Alternative Room is located adjacent to the study hall and regular study hall teachers supervise both the regular students and those assigned to the Alternative Room. Responsibilities for students placed in the Alternative Room are spelled out clearly in writing. Parents sign an agreement indicating that they understand the restrictions and rules and will support the school in its expectation of acceptable behavior (see sample below). The basic thrust of the program is to provide the student with an opportunity to make up and/or keep current with school work. Reports indicate that most parents prefer this type of suspension to exclusion from school.

(Sample)

**NOTICE OF PLACEMENT OF STUDENT
IN CJHS ALTERNATIVE ROOM
AND EXPLANATION OF PROGRAM**

To:_____

    Your _____, _____ has been
        (son/daughter)
placed in our Alternative Room for a period of _____ days.

He/she will be released to return to his/her regular schedule
on _____.
(date)

During the period of time the student is in the Alternative Room, he/she is expected to report to the school office daily by 8:00 a.m. and will be released from school at 2:30 p.m. at which time he/she will be expected to leave the school premises and be on his/her way home.

The student will be expected to stay in the Alternative Room except for lunch time and will not be allowed to use his/her hall locker. Interaction with other students will be quite limited.

Teachers will provide the student with assignments and he/she is expected to keep busy working on them throughout the day. Adequate supervision and academic assistance will be provided so that he/she can keep up with schoolwork. The student will be expected to be courteous and to display a cooperative attitude at all times. He/she will comply with the rules of conduct established for the Alternative Room. If the student fails to work on assignments and/or displays unacceptable behavior, he/she will be sent home for at least the remainder of the suspension period.

Please detach, sign, and return to CJHS office.

I have read the explanation of the CJHS Alternative Room and understand the terms and responsibilities which are thereby placed on my child. I agree to support the school in its effort to provide this alternative for my child and in the restrictions it places on his/her school activities. I further understand that failure by my child to comply with these restrictions will result in his/her being sent home.

_____
Parent Signature

In addition to the varied forms of in-house suspension, discipline-minded schools throughout the country have selected from a wide wardrobe of other positive measures for improving behavior. The following sampling of successful programs and projects (actions plans) illustrates the broad spectrum of possibilities for making discipline better in any school.

Project "R"

At Pleasant View (IA) Elementary School, Project "R" (Respect, Responsibility, Reason, Reliability, and Real Living), a schoolwide project involving all staff members and students, has become standard operating procedure. In this ongoing program a variety of activities is designed to engage all parties affected in furthering respect and responsibility for self, for school, and for others. At least 60 minutes a week is devoted to classroom discussions on the emphasized activities and on respect/responsibility in general. Project "R" is intended to be more than a set of rules, activities, lesson plans, and consequences. Its ultimate purpose is to generate a feeling that permeates the entire school in order to make it a better place to learn, to teach, and to work.

Student Work Detail

LaPalma Junior High School (Buena Vista, CA) has received extensive recognition for its work program developed for those discipline cases where no threat to the welfare of students, staff or the school is involved. Under this approach, after school jobs are assigned to offenders. Possible work assignments include gardening, landscaping, custodial chores, clerical jobs, etc. An attempt is made to relate each assignment to the offense involved.

600 Synthesized Ideas on Self-Concept

In 1979, the Rosemount (MN) School District devoted one entire workshop day to the sharing of ideas on enhancing pupil self-concept. More than 600 teachers, administrators, and other licensed personnel shared papers describing successful teaching experiences and techniques related to self-concept development. The papers were then synthesized into a single handbook made available to all staff members. The workshop provided a quick and easy way to provide all teachers with a comprehensive, ready reference of tested tips for improving student self-esteem and helping students to become mature, responsible school citizens.

Choice—Not Chance

The Lincoln Choice—Not Chance program in the Seattle (WA) Public Schools reflects recognition that teaching and learning styles differ. Six educational options are offered to provide students a chance to choose an approach to learning staffed by teachers who themselves have chosen the same approach. The goal is to develop smaller communities of students and teachers with commonalities in preference of educational styles. The options available include:

a. Academic emphasis
b. Careers
c. Regular school
d. Adaptability community
e. Student directed community
f. Small group learning

A significant aspect of the program is that these options are designed to be available to students in their own high school—not some place apart.

Counselor-Teacher Approach to Classroom Management

A number of Austin (TX) elementary schools have adopted a counselor-teacher approach to classroom management for grades K-5. This program attempts to "turn around" classrooms with severe discipline problems by introducing a climate involving students more directly in the learning process and in achieving responsible behavior. Emphasis is placed on the consultative and participating roles of the school counselor in working with the teacher in the regular classroom.

"G.O.A.L.S." Program

The objectives of the G.O.A.L.S. project (*Goals Offer Adolescents Learning Success*), an adjunct program in the St. Louis Park (MN) Public Schools include:

a. Intervening with behaviorally disruptive/socially irresponsible students; and

b. Helping students to set goals, work on goals, and reach goals.

The program is designed for junior-senior high students with special learning/behavior problems experiencing difficulties in school. Methods utilized in the G.O.A.L.S. approach include goal attainment scaling; learning theory approach/behavior therapy; rational emotive therapy; and individual/group sessions.

County Learning Center

The Ann Arundel County Learning Center in Maryland offers a short-term program (minimum time of one semester) for students who must be temporarily removed from school because of behavior problems either in or out of school. Self-discipline lies at the core of the program. Parents of students involved in the Center are provided with a Parent Resource Program kit containing an explanation of the program and practical information on parenting. The Learning Center relies heavily on a logical consequences system whereby students may earn daily certificates for good work and proper behavior.

Adaptability Emphasis Program

The Adaptability Emphasis Program in the Seattle (WA) Public Schools is aimed at grades 4-5. The program is designed around a recognition of individuality and differences in learning styles. The primary goal is to help children achieve responsible self-direction. Heavy emphasis is placed on learning how to learn.

Second Start

The target group for the Second Start program at Stillwater (MN) Senior High is the near-dropout and the behavior problem student. The program is designed to increase the chances of these students remaining in school by providing a specially arranged program, tutoring, and individual/group counseling (see Sample Group Counseling Goal-Setting Schedule below). Students in the program may be tutored in lieu of class attendance or tutoring may be in addition to regular classes. Positive results have been evidenced by a noticeable increase in attendance, grades, and attitudes toward school.

**SAMPLE GROUP COUNSELING
GOAL-SETTING SCHEDULE**

Instructions: At the time of beginning a group, many persons have goals for themselves in terms of changes they would like to make. Here are some statements of goals for the group made by members of other groups.

What changes do you personally feel you want to make on each item below? For each item, check the column that most clearly represents change you feel you want to make on that item. If you feel okay about yourself in an area, mark the "remain the same" answer. *Notice:* you may choose to increase or decrease certain kinds of behaviors and feelings.

Please Check One Column for Each Item

	I want to increase	I want to stay the same	I want to decrease
1. My self-consciousness			
2. My interest in other people			
3. My ability to make friends			
4. My ability to accept other people's ideas			
5. My understanding of myself			

Other goals not listed:

In the space below list three of your most important goals.

Note: Keep this goal-setting schedule. Look at it periodically to measure how you are achieving your goals.

Remember: The group is a place where you as an individual are accepted for who you are. If you are having some trouble changing the things you wish to, the group may be able to help. *Ask!*

Discipline Brochure in Spanish

The Onxard (CA) School District has improved school-home communications and support of the minority community by publishing its student discipline brochures in both English and Spanish (See Sample English-Spanish Discipline Brochure Excerpts below).

SAMPLE ENGLISH-SPANISH DISCIPLINE BROCHURE EXCERPTS

RESPONSIBILITY OF THE PUPIL AND PARENT	RESPONSABILIDAD DEL ALUMNO Y PADRE
Behavior of Pupils. Every pupil shall attend school punctually and regularly; conform to the regulations of the school; obey promptly all the directions of his teachers and others in authority; observe good order and propriety of deportment; be diligent in study; respectful to his teachers and others in authority; kind and courteous to schoolmates; and refrain entirely from the use of profane and vulgar language.	*Conducta de Alumnos.* Cada alumno debe asistir a la escuela puntualmente y regularmente; someterse a las regulaciones de la escuela; obedecer rapidamente todas las direcciones de su maestro y otros en autoridad; observar buen orden y propriedad de compartamiento; ser diligente en estudiar; respetuoso para su maestro y otros en autoridad; bondadoso y cortés para sus compañeros de escuela; y abstenerse completamente del uso de lenguaje profano y vulgar.

Student Conduct Committee

The Plymouth-Canton (MI) Community Schools have experienced success in establishing an active Student Conduct Committee. The makeup and function of the Committee are outlined in the following official school policy:

> *It shall be an administrative responsibility to establish a standing committee to be known as the Student Conduct Committee. The responsibility of this committee shall be to review issues or problems directed to it by the Executive Forum or by student petition. This committee will be a student committee with faculty and administrative representation. The power of the Student Conduct Committee shall proceed from the basic princi-*

ple of conference and compromise. The Student Conduct Committee may have conferences with the administration and faculty whenever any policy is being instituted or formulated by the administration. Students should be aware of these policies and their construction and institution.

Project Pride

As part of a district-wide anti-vandalism project, the Lawrence, (KS) Public Schools designate each October as *Project Pride Month* during which one week is celebrated as *Project Pride Week.* Special emphasis is placed on students participating in all phases of school cleanup. Students are rewarded for the smallest acts from tossing a can into a barrel, to picking up trash, to preventing vandalism. The Board of Education also gives each school a Project Pride Fund ($1.00 per pupil) for school improvements. This fund is reduced each time vandalism occurs in the school. An additional $600 is available to schools to carry out special Pride Projects. Schools submit proposals to compete for these annual grants. School vandalism has been significantly reduced during the several years that the program has been in operation.

Alternative programs and action plans, such as those discussed above, are not panaceas for disruptive behavior, but they do exemplify some creative beginnings for dealing with the problems facing schools. From a broader perspective, the remainder of this chapter profiles a number of schools that have put together a holistic approach to promoting behavioral health in the school setting.

SOME SCHOOLS THAT HAVE MADE A DIFFERENCE IN DISCIPLINE

Despite public perceptions, media messages, and Gallup Polls to the contrary, a vast number of American public schools are aware of the discipline situation and are conducting the business of education in an orderly and productive atmosphere. The thumbnail sketches that follow represent these reasonably good, peaceful schools, which can become the standard everywhere. Each of the following schools has achieved some notable success in maintaining desirable discipline and a positive learning climate.

Columbus (NB) Junior High School

At Columbus Jr. High, the staff has adopted a Student Management Team approach to improving student behavior. Simply stated, this approach defines the school's communication/problem-solving process. This "nonpower" means of resolving difficult situations is based on the premise that student management problems are best solved at the lowest perceived level of authority. Thus, the fundamental goal of the program is to ensure that teachers take clear-cut, initial responsibility for disciplining the students under their supervision. The Columbus process involves the following progressive levels of communication and problem solving:

a. Teacher-pupil (on a personal level)

b. Teacher-pupil-parent

c. Teacher-pupil-parent-counselor

d. Teacher-pupil-parent-counselor-administrator

Since the inception of the Student Management Team concept, the number of individual students referred to the administration for discipline reasons has decreased 23 percent.

Chester W. Nimitz Jr. High School (Huntington Park, CA)

Following the pattern of long established academic honors societies, Nimitz Jr. High has built its discipline program, in part, around the establishment of a *Citizenship Honors Society*. The society serves as a focal point for the school's total efforts toward behavior betterment. Requirements for selection to the society include reliability, cooperation, and positive work habits. Special activities are planned as a reward for the membership of the society.

St. Anthony Village (MN) High School

St. Anthony Village High School has achieved marked progress in bringing about a positive structured school environment through the use of a *process approach* to discipline. An attempt is made to apply the process in a systematic way to all major discipline problems in the school. The particular problem-solving style, which has proved effective at St. Anthony Village, is based on the six action steps outlined below:

1. Investigation and diagnosis of causes of the problem.
2. Assessment of alternative solutions (with an emphasis on looking creatively for the third, fourth, or even fifth alternative).
3. Involvement of a variety of people associated with the problem.
4. Utilization of mediation, counterproposals, and compromise where necessary.
5. Analysis and selection of a proposed solution.
6. Thoughtful (well-planned) implementation of the proposed solution.

An overwhelming number of parents and teachers concur that school climate has improved since the introduction of the process-approach concept.

North Allegheny (PA) Public Schools

Since 1974, the North Allegheny Schools have focused a good deal of their discipline efforts at the secondary level on the establishment of a COPE Center for high school students who exhibit "norm-violating" behavior. COPE is an acronym for Counseling Opportunities in Personal Exploration. The emphasis in the Center is on exploring positive approaches to discipline by helping students to help each other. Over a six-year period, the success, acceptance, and stability of the Center have steadily increased.

The Gypsy School (Seattle, WA)

This specialized school in Seattle provides a basic-skills emphasis for elementary students. Heavy emphasis is also placed on the involvement of Gypsy parents. Many problems have been reduced or eliminated because the school fosters an atmosphere in which the students feel important, have a sense of belonging, and feel relatively free of undue academic frustration.

Park Terrace Elementary School (Spring Lake Park, MN)

The staff of the Park Terrace Elementary School has earned considerable attention through its successful efforts to restore classroom discipline to a difficult school situation. Much of their success is credited to the school's strong advisory program and frequent staffings. In the advisory program, each teacher acts as advisor to a homeroom of students who meet together three times daily. Each homeroom becomes involved in a number of problem-solving activities such as: rap sessions; incentive programs; self-esteem "roasts" (where students are bombarded with compliments for their strengths and achievements); value clarification exercises; and individual student goal setting in the area of discipline.

Community School 102 (Bronx, NY)

Community School 102 in the Bronx has built its positive/preventive discipline program around a collection of 30 Practical Guidance Tips for Teachers. This set of guidance guidelines is designed to assist staff members in handling large group, as well as individual discipline situations. The compilation of these tips is used as the focal point of orientation and inservice for the school staff each year.

Monroe Extension Center (Cedar Rapids, IA)

This junior high Extension Center offers an educational program for students in grades 7-9 who have been unable to adjust to a regular secondary school program. The effectiveness of the Center is partially attributable to its size (maximum of 50 students) and its family atmosphere (average class size of ten). Teachers at the Center emphasize individual growth; thus, the goals are not the same for every student. One common goal does exist for all students, however—eventual return to a regular school program. The length of the school day has been planned with the unique nature of the Extension Center's pupils in mind ... their needs, their lifestyles, and their tolerance for structured activity. Attendance is required Monday through Thursday and Friday is an optional attendance day.

Killian Senior High School (Miami, FL)

As part of the educational-discipline program at Killian Senior High, all students participate in a required mini-course dealing with assault and disruptive behavior. "Learning Pacs" used in the course include information on the consequences of various forms of misbehavior and specific steps for reporting violations.

Ridgemount Junior High (Wayzata, MN)

Ridgemount Jr. High has developed a well-rounded program of integrated discipline measures that work together to successfully manage student behavior. The Ridgemount approach includes the elements outlined below:

- *Support Team Concept*—Specialized personnel are organized into a support team whose purpose is to provide teachers, parents, and students with assistance in problem areas.
- *Discipline Philosophy*—A schoolwide philosophy based on behavior counseling and preexamination of choices and consequences.
- *In-School Suspension*—Designed for two basic admission periods: hourly/daily or for a number of days.
- *Crisis Room*—A "cooling off" spot for major problems arising during the school day.
- *Learning Center Program*—An alternative approach for educating pupils who do not meet the behavioral expectations of mainstream education.
- *Progression of Services*—Designed to keep track of a student's alternative programming and future possibilities.

Centennial Elementary (Lawrence, KS)

Intermediate grade discipline at Centennial Elementary School has been improved through implementation of a point system program for self-discipline. Under this approach, every student begins each nine-week period with 100 points. Points are removed if and when infractions occur. A grid chart of each student's status is maintained by each homeroom teacher in a location where the students may check their point totals at anytime. Although no pupil can accrue more than 100 points, students may make up lost points by doing things to help the school. At the conclusion of the quarter, a school assembly is held to present Self-Discipline Awards to all who have retained 94-100 points. Usually about 95 percent of the students in each intermediate classroom receive the award.

Kearney (NB) Jr. High School

The most important component of the student management program at Kearney Jr. High is a committee approach to discipline enforcement. Six faculty members serve on the schoolwide Discipline Committee along with the assistant principal. The Committee conducts major infraction hearings whenever needed. In addition, the Committee has established specific consequences for common behavior problems. The primary focus, however, is on changing the behavior pattern of the student before he/she gets into any serious trouble.

All of the dropout prevention programs, action plans, and model schools profiled in this chapter exemplify the positive discipline principles and practices emphasized throughout this handbook. Additional details and information on any of the programs described above may be obtained by contacting the particular school or district involved.

As a special feature, the next short chapter treats one of the most sensitive gray areas of discipline confronting and confounding many modern schools—the problems of teenage pregnancy and venereal disease (VD).

9

Special Help on Teenage Pregnancy and VD

UNDERSTANDING THE DIMENSIONS OF THE PROBLEM

Educators, as well as the entire adult society in general, are becoming increasingly alarmed by the growing incidence of early teenage sexual activity and the resultant epidemic of consequences, including proliferating pregnancies and an explosion of venereal disease.

Similar to the pattern of drug usage, the average age of initial sexual exposure and experimentation has consistently gone down throughout the last two decades. Sexual activity among 12 to 14 year olds is now not uncommon in this country.

Early introduction to sexual behavior is not confined to any racial, social, or economic subculture—rather, it is pervasive throughout the adolescent population. The causes of earlier sexual activity appear to be rooted in the shifting cultural patterns that characterize our modern society. These include:

1. Earlier maturation
2. Increased sexual orientation throughout the culture
3. Mixed messages from society concerning sanctioned and tabooed sexual behavior
4. Diminished nuclear family structures
5. The emergence of alternative lifestyles

6. A daily deluge of sex-oriented stimuli (e.g., music, fashions, literature, media, etc.)

7. Lowered age of majority

8. Expanded teenage mobility and privacy

9. An overly protracted period of forced nonproductivity for adolescents

10. Teenage isolation and loneliness (Many young people are literally "stranded" in the present and virtually live "alone" at home.)

The two primary consequences of this early sexual experimentation, pregnancy and VD, are devastating and lifelong. Both of these consequences are currently compounded by gross ignorance on the part of an enormous number of youth throughout the nation concerning the biology of conception, contraception, and the potential ravages of venereal disease.

In the eyes of many public health officials, the rampant spread of VD among teenagers is a national disaster. Equally damaging, however, are the lifelong ramifications of early pregnancy noted below.

THE PRICE OF ADOLESCENT PREGNANCY

- High risk of medical complications for both mother and child (e.g., toxemia, premature delivery, low birth weight, etc.).

- Greater than average mortality rates for infants of teenage mothers.

- Repeated pregnancies. (Teen mothers tend to give birth to approximately twice as many children as women who defer childbearing.)

- Interrupted or terminated schooling.

- High divorce rates/unstable families.

- Limited economic horizons. (A malproportion of adolescent mothers never rise above the poverty level and live out their lives as welfare wards.)

- High suicide rate. (The incidence of suicide among teen mothers is many times higher than the national norm.)

The bottom line of the current adolescent sex scene is simply that for many young people, the modern "Great American Tragedy" is the story of teenage marriage prefaced by illegitimate pregnancy, destined for divorce.

The advent of adolescent sexual awakening is a delicate, sensitive, and awkward period for both teenagers and their parents and consequently, for the school itself. Teen sex, pregnancy, and VD constitute an unusual gray area of behavior and discipline for school personnel. Adolescent sexual activity and its potentially catastrophic results are not school discipline problems in the same sense as vandalism, truancy, or drug use on school premises. Most student sexual behavior does not occur at school during regular school time. No prohibitive or punitive policy/action on the part of the school seems particularly appropriate or holds much promise of being effective.

In addition, the whole area of adolescent sexual activity constitutes a catch-22 situation for concerned teachers and administrators. Many parents would like for the school to do something about teen sex; but many other parents and even more teenagers feel equally as strongly, and with some legitimate logic, that it is none of the school's business.

Nevertheless, teenage pregnancy and VD are real problems that directly affect learning, student health and safety, school climate, and morale, as well as public confidence and support. Thus, the public school cannot conscientiously ignore these critical social issues. What then should school personnel do? The remainder of this chapter provides some answers to this question by spotlighting a variety of distinct means that the school community can undertake to reduce the damage of early sexual experimentation.

WHAT THE SCHOOL CAN DO ABOUT ADOLESCENT PREGNANCY AND VD

In most states, there are no laws or standards that govern the education of pregnant students. As a result, confusion and lack of uniformity characterize practices throughout the country. Despite the lack of common direction, and the highly sensitive atmosphere that surrounds teenage sexual behavior, schools are not helpless and should not remain passive. Obviously, no policy will prohibit and no punishment will curtail adolescent sexual activity. Nevertheless, there are many things that school officials can do regarding the problems of pregnancy and VD, which are positive, practical and proactive. The suggestions that follow represent measures that can and have produced beneficial results:

- Avoid the self-fulfilling prophecy of belittling adolescents as irresponsible *children*. (If teenagers are not treated as adults or near adults, their behavior will almost inevitably be childish—characterized by the kind of defiance and thrill-seeking that can lead to irresponsible sexual behavior.)

- Avoid adding to the hype about sex. (Don't encourage any activities that tend to flaunt sex.)

- Refrain from assuming that all pregnant students are bad. (Avoid a tone or approach that conveys guilt.)

- Extend all possible help to assure that the education of pregnant students is not ended or overly interrupted.

- Stress better parent-teen communication in every possible way.

- Adopt/enact official school policies that protect the rights of pregnant students, guarantee effective educational programs for these students, and legitimize proper and acceptable instruction relating to human sexuality for all students. (See the three sample policies below.)

Sample Policy #1

PREGNANT STUDENTS

Pregnant students shall have the opportunity to continue in the regular program, to receive homebound instruction, or to attend a Continuing Education Center.

Sample Policy #2

PREGNANT AND MARRIED STUDENTS

Rosemount, (MN) Public Schools

a. Marital, maternal, or parental status shall not affect the rights and privileges of students to receive a public education nor to take part in any extracurricular activity offered by the school.

b. Pregnant students shall be permitted to continue in school in all instances unless the physician of the expectant mother deems school attendance not advisable. The school administration is authorized to make special arrangements for the instruction of pregnant students and to provide an educational program designed to meet their special needs.

c. The student is entitled to receive homebound instruction prior to delivery and for a reasonable time after delivery. The homebound instruction will be delivered at the rate of one hour of instruction per day of absence.

Sample Policy #3

SEX EDUCATION

The professional staff shall establish and provide within the K-12 curriculum programs of instruction relating to sex education.

The instructional materials used shall be reviewed annually by the appropriate staff to assure authenticity and accuracy. When necessary, the staff shall cooperate with and seek the assistance of appropriate public and private agencies as well as competent and knowledgeable individuals available in the community.

Parents and other citizens shall be permitted to review and observe all materials used in instruction in these areas upon request.

Except where required by law, students may be excused by the teacher from participating in these special areas of instruction upon written parental request. In such cases, appropriate arrangement shall be made by the teacher for meaningful alternative programs of study.

- Ensure that students are provided with an adequate, appropriate and meaningful program of sex education *either in school or elsewhere.* If provided in school, the program should include elective courses (e.g., human sexuality, human growth/development, family living, etc.), as well as integrated units in established courses. (See the next section of this chapter.)

• Provide appropriate program alternatives for pregnant girls. Ideally, such programs should encompass a combination of traditional study along with training in prenatal and infant care, household management, etc., within the school framework if possible. (See Profile of a Special High School for Pregnant Students.)

**PROFILE OF A SPECIAL HIGH SCHOOL
FOR PREGNANT STUDENTS**

Continuing Education Center
Hennepin County (MN) Area
Vocational-Technical Schools

1. Operated in an apartment setting separate from the regular school.
2. Guided by a broad-based advisory committee.
3. Students complete courses needed to graduate.
4. Professional nurses visit the school periodically and the students visit hospitals during the course of the program.
5. Parents enter into *commitment contracts* (e.g., to give their pregnant child four hugs daily).
6. Lessons revolve around individualized learning pacs stressing specific objectives.
7. Students learn:
   a. child care
   b. the responsibility, trauma, and satisfaction of being a parent
   c. to be comfortable with themselves
   d. to make bid decisions
   e. to make the best of unexpected situations
   f. to eat wisely
   g. to shop wisely
   h. to be economically independent

- Ensure that pregnant students (married or unmarried) are not discriminated against and have full access to all programs, activities, and services of the school.

- Guarantee special attention to an effective health education program for all students focused on venereal disease (see later section in this chapter).

- Establish an effective program of "parenting" education. (See Chapter 7.)

- Ensure that all teenagers have easy access to the information (e.g., biological data, alternatives for pregnant girls), referral sources (e.g., clinics, treatment centers) and services (e.g., family counseling, pregnancy testing) that they may need, either in school or elsewhere in the community.

- Encourage media awareness of the problems of adolescent pregnancy and VD.

- Establish and/or participate in a Community Family Planning/Education Council.

- Make provision for pregnant students to leave school and to be readmitted with no adverse status, penalty, or stigma on their record. (Eliminate any arbitrarily required waiting period before a pregnant student or teen mother can return to school.)

- Establish appropriate peer group support systems.

- Utilize Community Education services to provide special activities and assistance to adolescent parents including childcare classes, nutrition education, family management instruction, expectant father courses, counseling, etc.

- Make available a program of transition counseling aimed at meeting the needs of young people as they become adults. Such programs should include:
  a. group settings in which teens can share the agony and ecstasy of achieving adulthood.
  b. work with adolescents regarding their individual/personal sexual development.
  c. pregnancy counseling.

Transition counseling can be conducted by professionals or volunteers and may be offered in the school or on location in homes, churches, other youth agency facilities, etc.

- Lobby for effective legislation and funding geared to the needs of pregnant students and teen parents (e.g., teen clinics, preventive programs, etc.).
- Actively support a *total* community program for pregnant girls and teen parents, which includes the programs and services listed below:
  a. Quality medical care with emphasis on the special needs of pregnant students.
  b. Opportunities for continuing basic education.
  c. Supplemental education programs (e.g., consumerism, infant care, etc.).
  d. Day care.
  e. Vocational training/job placement.
  f. Counseling (including career guidance). Special emphasis should be placed on helping pregnant students to clarify options and make decisions.
  g. Financial aid.
- Consider establishing family planning clinics directly in the high school where feasible. Staffing may include medical social worker(s), nurse practitioner(s), and clinic attendant(s). Where they have been tried, such clinics have been most successful if other health services are also provided by the clinic (e.g., physical examinations, immunizations, weight control, etc.). The St. Paul (MN) Public Schools experienced a 40 percent reducation in pregnancy among students in two schools through the use of this kind of on-site clinic.

From the long view, the cornerstone of any community's commitment to reducing adolescent pregnancy and VD must be a sound program of factually founded sex education if all children and youth are to benefit. Despite a recurring plethora of local controversies in some areas, in many places the most effective focal point for such a program is the school.

The next section traces the basic elements for initiating and conducting a program of sex education that serves the needs of young people and satisfies community standards and expectations.

ESSENTIALS OF A SUCCESSFUL
SEX EDUCATION PROGRAM

Admittedly, any program of sex education in school is a highly charged and sensitive subject for many parents and citizens. In almost every instance where a school-based program has been introduced, school authorities receive varying degrees of heat and flak. Nevertheless, repeated polls and studies have established that most people favor sex education in school—including the teaching about contraceptive methods. The experience of countless districts throughout the United States has revealed the following hard core of truth:

1. Sex education in school does *not* increase sexual behavior among teenagers;
2. Such programs seem to improve teen-parent communication; and
3. Where controversies have erupted, most programs have been expanded, rather than eliminated.

It serves no purpose for school personnel to deny that sex education is, and should be, principally the prerogative of the home. Unfortunately, however, most sex education (or miseducation) is currently taught somewhere between the home and the school—most commonly by peers!

In the light of documented widespread ignorance regarding conception, contraception, and venereal disease among teenagers; an appalling proliferation of adolescent pregnancies; and a growing epidemic of VD among young people; school officials must feel an obligation to promote sound sex education.

If the climate of public tolerance will not permit sex education within the school framework, teachers and administrators should become assertive advocates of improved programs elsewhere (e.g., the home, the church, outside youth agencies, etc.). Where community support is available, however, the best long-range solution for problems of teen pregnancy and VD lies in a reasonable, well-rounded program of school-based sex education. The conditions and components necessary for providing such a program are outlined below.

BASICS OF AN EFFECTIVE SCHOOL-BASED SEX EDUCATION PROGRAM		
Instructional Objectives	**Teacher Attitudes and Attributes**	**Teaching Strategies and Techniques**
To provide accurate information concerning the physiology of sex and the causes and effects of venereal disease	Sensitivity/tolerance	Avoid setting rules or dictating standards
	Knowledgeable and well-informed	Utilize a *discovery* (inquiry) approach
	Full understanding of human growth and development characteristics	Provide for student anonymity in asking sensitive questions (e.g., use a Question Box)
To foster positive student self-images		
To assist students in understanding sexual feelings	Ability to handle delicate and sometimes, disconcerting topics	
	Comfortableness with the assignment	Respect confidentialities
To prepare students for personal decision making	Ability to remain nonjudgmental	Avoid scare tactics and sermonizing
To promote sexually responsible behavior	Interest and involvement in student activities	Provide for a balance of coeducational and sex-segregated instruction
To provide preparation for familial roles		
To foster emotional maturity (coping capacity)	Self-acceptance/ sense of self-worth (ability to give of self in order to help students develop their own self-identities)	Respect individual differences and beliefs
To engender respect for human sexuality		Keep parents fully informed of the program

Where sex education programs have been most successful and well accepted in schools, certain elements have usually been present. The success factors shared by these effective systems include the following:

Characteristics of Successful Sex Education Programs

- Use of a citizen-staff planning/advisory committee as a first step. (Most such committees include representatives of the PTA, the clergy, and the medical community, as well as appropriate staff members.)

- Community support (parent/public pressure or backing will make or break the program).
- Administrative support and commitment. (This must include the School Board and must entail more than lip service.)
- Sequential programming. (The best programs are introduced early and provide coordinated instruction on a K-12 basis.)
- Comfortable, competent teachers (a *must*).
- Availability of separate elective courses as well as provision of integrated units within existing courses.
- Provision of opportunities for students to opt out of the program. (No child should be compelled to participate in the sex education program if parents object.)
- Up-to-date materials.
- Strict adherence to district policy.

Regardless of the disagreements that may arise regarding many aspects of the school's sex education program, (e.g., information about conception, contraception, abortion, homosexuality, etc.), there is one area that serves as a rallying point for conservatives, moderates, and liberals alike—*all* students must learn the facts about VD. The last section of this chapter lays out step-by-step procedures for conducting a vigorous anti-VD program within the school.

HARDHITTING VD CONTROL TECHNIQUES

Widespread venereal disease among teenagers is a social sore that must be healed. The public school cannot shirk its responsibility for making a major contribution to society's attack on this critical public health problem.

Knowledge about VD may or may not reduce adolescent sexual experimentation. It can, however, have significant impact in curbing one of America's major communicable disease crises. The ten-point action plan described below can be used by any school staff (large or small) to institute measures to minimize VD among students.

A Ten-Point VD Action Program

1. Insist on a comprehensive, vital VD health education curriculum. (Regardless of whatever community controversy or sensitivity may surround sex education in general, the school must have a no-nonsense program of instruction related to venereal disease. See Sample Objectives.)

SAMPLE OBJECTIVES FOR VD EDUCATION

- Gain knowledge of the historical, medical, epidemiological, and social aspects of VD.
- Understand the causes, effects, prevention, transmission, recognition, and treatment of venereal disease.
- Understand preventive health measures, as well as control measures.
- Develop a scientific understanding of the VD problem.
- Appreciate community and individual responsibility for control.
- Dispel unscientific and unfounded fears, myths, misconceptions, and misinformation regarding VD.

---

2. Conduct an active parent awareness program. Avoid soft-pedaling the seriousness of the problem. A variety of channels may be employed in such a communication campaign including the following:

- PTSA meetings
- Cable television
- Mailings (fact sheets)

- Local media
- Mobile City Hall
- Cassettes and video tapes available for home check out

3. Urge the medical community and local health department officials to compile a community profile on the incidences of VD and to release this information to the public on a periodic basis.

4. Require physical examinations for participation in the school's athletic program. (A minimum program would require such an examination every three years.)

5. Provide thorough inservice training regarding VD for all counselors, health instructors, nurses, and other school health personnel.

6. Call upon local health department officials to serve as classroom resource persons and consultants to the staff.

7. Encourage the PTSA and other civic groups to sponsor a hot line (a first first call for help) that would be available to both students and parents seeking information or help regarding venereal disease or other problems.

8. Establish an active liaison with all appropriate social service and youth-serving agencies.

9. Maintain an information booth in the school where a variety of materials concerning referral sources, VD signs, drug information, and other problems are available to students in a low-key manner.

10. Promote total cooperation with the public health department in identifying, reporting, and tracking cases of VD involving teenagers.

The public school is not the cause of accentuated and accelerated early sexual experimentation, increased adolescent pregnancies, or the cancerous spread of VD within the teenage population. Neither can the school singlehandedly reverse these trends or eliminate the problems.

Nevertheless, school officials can and should exert assertive leadership in mobilizing every means possible to minimize the dangers and to equip young people to cope with the so-called sexual revolution. This chapter has offered a variety of bold, simple techniques for fulfilling this role.

As a *minimum,* every school should be committed on two points:

1. To guarantee the right of all students to know their rights regarding the confidentiality of diagnosis, treatment, medical records, etc.

2. To ensure that all students know or can readily find out where to get information and help when needed on a confidential basis.

The following final chapter of this handbook offers a succinct synthesis of the down-to-earth, affirmative approach to discipline stressed throughout the text. This concluding material also includes some provocative added survival hints and helps in maintaining positive student behavior in any school.

10

More Help for Discipline Problems
—a Final Word

This handbook is based on the following fundamental premises derived from the experiences of successful schools in all parts of the country:

a. A productive school atmosphere based on reasonable control is absolutely essential to the purpose of education.

b. Discipline in most schools is better than most people think it is. Unfortunately, some problems and horror stories, which happen relatively infrequently, have become distorted through publicity overkill.

c. Positive discipline is achievable in any school.

d. Positive discipline is not produced by piecemeal punishment. A holistic approach that promotes prevention affords the safest and surest course to better behavior in our schools.

e. The school is an ecosystem that relies on *balance* and *interdependence*. As such, all of the key actors involved (e.g., students, teachers, administrators, parents, etc.), must contribute to the establishment of an orderly environment. Most people (students and adults alike) want some structure in the learning milieu that can be attained only through an active participatory partnership.

There is no question that the public school students of today are more assertive, demanding, rights-oriented, and questioning than pupils in the past. Consequently, many measures that worked in earlier times are now of limited value and often generate waves of alienation and outrage that are counterproductive to the goals of good discipline.

This handbook points out viable alternatives to some of these shop-worn, traditional discipline approaches and equips educational personnel with an inventory of psychologically proven control techniques that can meet the needs of today's school.

This final chapter presents additional resources that are available to teachers and principals in creating or in restoring a positive school climate, as well as specific suggestions on how to keep on top of the situation once sound discipline has been established.

HOW TO KEEP CONTROL
ONCE YOU'VE GOT IT

Contrary to popular conventional wisdom, school authorities are not immune to the foibles of human nature. Consequently, complacency can become a real enemy in sustaining school control. Through neglect or smug self-satisfaction, it is possible for a healthy, peaceful school to deteriorate into an abyss of anarchy and lack of control within a short period.

To succeed in maintaining optimum discipline requires sustained effort, ongoing attention, and continual vigilance. The following is a collection of 16 important maintenance measures that can help the school to "keep a good thing going" and to ensure the continuation of control once a proper atmosphere has been developed.

1. Teachers and administrators must "earn their wings" by establishing authority and credibility *every day*. The steps described in this handbook are not once-only measures, but must become part of the ongoing, regular routine of running the school.

2. The school staff must consistently avoid modeling any form of aggressive, abusive, or dehumanizing behavior.

3. Major attention should be devoted to the continual finetuning of the curriculum through review, evaluation,

and change. The goal is a fluid program that is loaded with options. The curriculum should be formed to fit students, rather than being shaped to conform to the length of class periods or the format of the school day. Too often, problem students receive modified programming only after they rebel and are in a serious disciplinary situation.

4. Shared decision making should be practiced in all aspects of operating the school.

5. All communication should be open, frequent, direct, and two-way.

6. Care should be exercised to honor student privacy and confidentiality and to provide young people with personal space.

7. The school staff should strive to reward those students who obey the rules. The successful school maximizes positive attention to productive behavior and seeks to minimize negative attention to unacceptable behavior.

8. Inservice training on modern discipline techniques and strategies should be provided for all staff members (teachers, custodians, food service personnel, etc.), on a periodic basis. A surprising number of well-trained, experienced teachers have received little, if any, direct instruction on classroom management. (See the sample course outline below.)

**SAMPLE OUTLINE FOR TYPICAL INSERVICE
COURSE ON DISCIPLINE FOR TEACHERS**

- Philosophy and purpose of discipline
- Child and adolescent psychology: selected topics
- Essentials of learning theory
- Cultural and ethnic behavioral differences

- Environmental concerns (aesthetics, room arrangement, etc.)
- Modeling appropriate behavior
- The *Halo Effect*
- Value clarification
- Eye contact
- Touch control

- Motivational techniques
- Competition and cooperation
- Reward and punishment
- The all-important self concept
- The "Rosenthal Thesis"
- Peer Pressure
- Praise Power and positive reinforcement
- Setting standards and establishing limits
- Democratic decision making
- A bill of rights for students
- Teaching styles— Learning styles
- Individualized instruction and personalized penalties
- Basic communication skills
- Active listening
- Planned discipline responses

- Behavior modification
- Performance contracts
- Corporal punishment: pros and cons
- Some promising practices
- The eclectic approach
- Handling hard-core cases
- Help is available
- The parent connection
- Liability and legal responsibility
- Teacher sanity/ stress reduction
- The futility of guilt
- The goal: self-directed discipline

9. Special attention should be devoted to the early identification of students with severe learning problems, potential dropouts, pupils exhibiting delinquent behavior, chronic troublemakers, and troubled students in general.

10. An active outreach program should be conducted on an ongoing basis to gain parent involvement and support and to provide needed training for parents.

11. A systematic effort should be exerted to collect accurate data on discipline in the school. The information needed to chart direction and redirection of staff's discipline program includes data on attendance, dropout statistics, and incidence and nature of offenses committed within the school. It is also important to assess the current beliefs and practices of those staff members responsible for student management and to evaluate the overall effectiveness of the school's discipline measures.

One helpful tool available to school personnel is a *Beliefs on Discipline Inventory* developed by Carl Blickman (University of Georgia) and Roy Tamashiro (Ohio State University). This inventory is a short, self-administered, self-scored instrument designed to arrive at a general assessment of an individual teacher's beliefs on discipline. The information gathered through the instrument can assist classroom teachers in taking stock of "where they're at" regarding student management, as well as permitting the chief administrator to gain an overall perspective of how the faculty culture within the school views behavior and discipline.

The Topeka (KS) Public Schools have also developed a useful device for surveying attitudes of professional staff members concerning discipline at both the district and building levels. This survey instrument, which can be adapted for use in any system, is reprinted here.

**A STUDY CONCERNING DISCIPLINE IN THE
TOPEKA PUBLIC SCHOOLS**

Section I: Professional data (Fill in information. Name is not necessary.)

A. Teaching Level (Circle one)

Elementary	Special Education
Junior High	Other (including administrators)
High School	_____

B. Area (Circle one):   A   B   C

C. If administrator, list title:_____

D. Years of teaching and/or administrative experience: _____

Section II: Indicate your evaluation of *The Philosophy of Discipline* as outlined in Policy 10200 of *The Topeka Plan*. (Refer to your copy.)

Topic	Strongly Support	Tend to Support	Cannot Support
A. Basic Nature of Discipline	_____	_____	_____
B. Importance of Good Discipline	_____	_____	_____
C. Discipline Procedures Must Be in Accordance with Good Educational Practices and Due Process	_____	_____	_____
D. Punishment Is Sometimes Necessary	_____	_____	_____
E. Suspension and Expulsion	_____	_____	_____
F. Definition of Terms—Corporal Punishment	_____	_____	_____
G. Definition of Terms—Restraint	_____	_____	_____
H. Rules and Regulations—Legal Authority for Suspension and Expulsion	_____	_____	_____
I. Rules and Regulations—Acts of Behavior Considered Unacceptable	_____	_____	_____
J. Rules and Regulations—Corporal Punishment	_____	_____	_____
K. Rules and Regulations—Procedures to be Followed with Pupils Who Have School Behavior Problems that May Lead to Suspension or Expulsion	_____	_____	_____
L. Rules and Regulations—Specific Rules and Regulations Governing Short-Term Suspensions	_____	_____	_____
M. Rules and Regulations—Specific Rules and Regulations for Extended Suspension and Expulsion Beyond a Period of Five School Days	_____	_____	_____
N. Rules and Regulations—Procedures for Appeal from Extended Suspension or Expulsion	_____	_____	_____

*Suggestions for change may be made on reverse side of this sheet.

Section III: Indicate your evaluation of correctional methods used in dealing with disciplinary cases.

	Of Much Value	Of Some Value	Of Little Value	Not Applicable at my Level
A. Keeping in before or after school	_____	_____	_____	_____

B. Keeping before or after school in detention status with rotating teachers in charge   _____ _____ _____ _____

C. Writing of sentences or selective words in responses to misdeed   _____ _____ _____ _____

D. Taking away privileges   _____ _____ _____ _____

E. Isolation for a period of time   _____ _____ _____ _____

F. Corporal punishment in accordance with provisions of *Topeka Plan*   _____ _____ _____ _____

G. Being sent home if agreement with parent (for balance of day)   _____ _____ _____ _____

H. Formal suspension   _____ _____ _____ _____

I. Loss of participation in extracurricular activities   _____ _____ _____ _____

J. Sitting it out to "cool off"   _____ _____ _____ _____

K. Use of special tutor in cases of excessive disruption (short time stay with adult tutor)   _____ _____ _____ _____

L. Counseling   _____ _____ _____ _____

M. Calling parents or guardians   _____ _____ _____ _____

N. Letter to parents or guardians   _____ _____ _____ _____

O. Home visit by teacher or administrator with or without student   _____ _____ _____ _____

P. Referral in professional manner to Special Services with teacher, administrator and parent

involvement and
agreement   _____ _____ _____ _____

Q. Referral to Juvenile
    Court   _____ _____ _____ _____

R. List others that you
    know of or utilize:

_____ _____ _____ _____ _____

_____ _____ _____ _____ _____

_____ _____ _____ _____ _____

_____ _____ _____ _____ _____

_____ _____ _____ _____ _____

_____ _____ _____ _____ _____

Section IV: Opinions Concerning Discipline

A. What do you consider the most critical disciplinary problems facing the
    Topeka Public Schools? (Be specific)

    1._____

    2._____

    3._____

B. What disciplinary measure(s) would you desire your building administrator
    utilize to a greater degree? (Classroom teacher only)

    _____

    _____

C. What disciplinary measure(s) would you desire your building administrator
    utilize to a lesser degree? (Classroom teacher only)

    _____

    _____

D. Please indicate the emphasis you think should be placed on the following
    listed subject areas to improve discipline and gain or maintain parental
    and patron support.

	Greater Emphasis	No Change in Emphasis	Less Emphasis
1. Improved communications from teachers to principal concerning discipline cases	_____	_____	_____

2. Improved communications from principal to teachers concerning action taken with discipline cases referred to the administrator   _____   _____   _____

3. House calls, telephone calls, letters from teachers and administrators to parents whose children may breech disciplinary standards   _____   _____   _____

4. More rapid involvement by Special Services in serious cases of student misconduct   _____   _____   _____

5. Use of written rules for each classroom (for use in classrooms where children can read)   _____   _____   _____

6. Other (list your views on the reverse side of this sheet.)

E. What type of in-service training could benefit you to improving discipline in your classroom or school?

_____

_____

F. Do you have suggestions on how to handle critical situations involving large numbers of students?

_____

_____

_____

G. This question is strictly limited to corporal punishment.

_____ I favor retention of corporal punishment in the Topeka Public Schools as presently outlined in the *Topeka Plan.*

_____ I favor forbidding corporal punishment in the Topeka Public Schools under any circumstances.

_____ I favor retention of corporation punishment in the Topeka Public Schools, but with following change as relates to the *Topeka Plan:*

_____

_____

_____

12. Even when the operation of the school is going well, staffs should continue to experiment with new discipline strategies and techniques. Adopting different procedures can sharpen the focus and attention of both students and staff on preemergent problems. Some schools have rejuvenated their discipline programs and renewed staff enthusiasm simply by trying fresh tactics such as establishing a *social seclusion room,* using *standouts* (where disruptive students are required to leave an ongoing activity briefly and face away toward a wall or other uninteresting view), or employing *timeouts* (removing violators temporarily from the vicinity of student activity), etc. Not every approach works, but many approaches are worth trying. Doing things differently can give teachers and principals a broader range of problem-solving tools and skills for future use.

13. The total staff should be continually watchful for signs of apathy, relaxed standards, or the gradual erosion of rules and positive behavior (see Symptoms of a Deteriorating School Climate below):

SYMPTOMS OF A DETERIORATING SCHOOL CLIMATE

- Inconsistency and teacher-administrator disagreement over discipline policy and practice
- Improper communication of school rules and expectations to parents and students
- Reliance on fear, verbal abuse, and/or physical punishment
- Procrastination in dealing with minor problems early—(a reactive, rather than a proactive approach to infractions)
- Existence of elitism or favoritism within the school
- Pervasive student boredom
- Preeminence of teacher-administrator concerns
- Lack of time and opportunity for the staff to collect information and mutually share ideas about discipline problems and policies
- Emphasis on group discipline and punishment

- Use of the curriculum as a weapon for control (e.g., extra homework, lower grades, etc.)
- An impersonal atmosphere within the school
- Tense relationships between and among student and adult groups in the school community

14. Try forming a cadre of leaders drawn from both the positive and negative segments of the student body who are trained to handle problem behavior in the school. Peer leadership can be a powerful tool for improving pupil attitude and action.

15. Responsible authorities should engage periodically in "what if" exercises to anticipate possible problems and alternative responses.

16. Continuing emphasis should be placed or positive punishments involving the loss of privileges that can be earned back by demonstrated improvement.

Regardless of what efforts are made to gain and retain control, there are always situations in which the staff needs support, consultation, or help from outside.

Teaching is too often perceived as an isolated profession. This need not be the case, however, if school personnel are aware of existing resources and are willing to reach out for the arsenal of assistance that is available to them.

The next section of this chapter catalogs a variety of helpful sources that can be tapped by any teacher or principal in dealing with many kinds of discipline problems.

WHERE TO LOOK FOR HELP
OUTSIDE THE SCHOOL

Discipline is not just a classroom problem—it is a schoolwide issue. Likewise, safe schools and the responsible behavior of young people are not just school matters, but are genuine concerns for the entire community and for society at large. Thus, achieving proper discipline should become a broad-based cooperative and collaborative venture.

Many aids are available to teachers and administrators in their quest for positive student behavior and a productive school climate. An effective staff eagerly seeks out and accepts such help from any and all legitimate sources.

Regardless of the size of the problem or whether it is an individual or a group concern, educators can often elicit valuable assistance, when needed, from the following types of ready-made resources:

1. Community groups and agencies
2. External organizations (e.g., social/governmental agencies, private and professional organizations, federal projects, commercial consulting firms)
3. Fellow professionals and concerned colleagues

Within every community, there are many groups, organizations, and agencies that can provide substantive support to the school, but that are often overlooked by the professional staff. A partial list of these potential community resources includes the following:

- Law enforcement agencies (e.g., police, sheriff, highway patrol)
- Juvenile court personnel (e.g., probation officer)
- PTSA
- Psychological clinics
- Legal Aid Society
- Health department
- Family counseling services
- Community centers
- Parent and/or child advocacy groups
- Teen clinics and treatment centers
- Service clubs
- Mental Health Society
- Religious organizations
- Department of Social Services
- Drug abuse centers
- Child Protection Agency

- Al-A-Teens
- Planned Parenthood Association
- Vocational Rehabilitation Services

In addition to the help at hand within the immediate community, there are a host of external private and public organizations that offer assistance to individual teachers, schools or school districts. The examples below represent a cross section of the variety of such sources from which schools can gain needed discipline help:

Educational Consulting Associates
P. O. Box 1515
Englewood, CO 80150

A well-known commercial consulting firm specializing in staff development seminars, conferences, audio-cassette courses and in-district programs on a variety of educational topics (e.g., Discipline—Practical, Constructive Techniques, Positive Classroom Climate—Effective Discipline Techniques, etc.)

Project T.E.A.C.H.
(Teacher Effectiveness and Classroom Handling)
Performance Learning Systems, Inc.
175 Westwood Ave.
Westwood, NJ 07675

An inservice course that offers viable solutions for modifying disruptive behaviors of students.

Educational Research Services, Inc.
1800 N. Kent Street
Arlington, VA 22209

A nonprofit agency that provides subscribing school personnel with timely research reports, abstracts of professional literature on specific subjects, and annotated bibliographies. Member districts may request individualized reports on any educational or discipline topic of interest.

Canter and Associates, Inc.
P. O. Box 64517
Los Angeles, CA 90064

A private consulting firm that offers staff workshops featuring a competency-based, take-charge approach to student management known as Assertive Discipline.

Learning Research and Development Center
3939 O'Hara Street
University of Pittsburgh
Pittsburgh, PA 15260

The stated mission of LRDC is to study and evaluate educational environments for elementary schools that are adaptive to individual students.

Wisconsin Research and Development
Center for Individualizing Schooling
University of Wisconsin—Madison
School of Education
1025 W. Johnson Street
Madison, WI 53706

WRDC promotes improved quality in education through individualized schooling. The center offers inservice and assistance to schools in implementing the popular Individualized Guided Education (IGE) program.

Eric Clearinghouse on Urban Education
Columbia University, Teachers College
Box 40
525 W. 120th Street
New York, NY 10027

The scope of the Clearinghouse encompasses structural changes in the classroom, school, system, and community, as well as other innovative instructional practices that directly affect urban students.

Project OUNCE
5110 Ashton Road
Sarasota, FL 33581

The project offers a structured alternative to authoritarian control involving 19 specific classroom management techniques. Training workshops are available at the OUNCE Center or at the adopter's site.

The National Center for the Study of
Corporal Punishment and Alternatives
in Schools
833 Ritter Hall South
Philadelphia, PA 19122

A national center dedicated to promoting alternatives to corporal punishment and to replacing physical abuse in schools with positive and preventive control measures.

In the eyes of many authorities, however, the most practical aid for dealing with discipline problems available to front-line practitioners can come only from experienced and concerned colleagues. Every teacher and administrator should strive to establish contacts and linkages with a variety of fellow professionals who are willing to share successful techniques and tested programs. Peer support can be a prime force in fostering effective leadership for improved student behavior and enhanced school climate.

The Discipline Duty Roster below represents a nationwide network of experienced educators concerned about discipline who have contributed many of the suggestions, exemplary practices, and sample procedures included in this handbook, and who stand ready to assist other professionals in maximizing positive behavior in all public schools.

A Discipline Duty Roster

(A national network of professional
educators concerned about discipline)

Jerry P. Allred
Director/Personnel
East Allen County Schools
1240 U. W. 30 E
New Haven, IN 46774

Paul Baarson, Principal
Parkview Elementary
ISD #196
14445 Diamond Path
Rosemount, MN 55068

David Bailey
Assistant Superintendent
Grand Rapids Public
  Schools
143 Bostwick Ave. NE
Grand Rapids, MI 49503

Dan Beal
Assistant Principal
Fairview Jr. High School
Roseville, MN 55113

David R. Bowden
Weedsport Central School
  System
Weedsport, NY 13166

Edward Buegmann,
  Principal
Hillcrest Elementary School
9301 Thomas Road
Bloomington, MN 55431

Knute Clark
South San Francisco
  Unified School District
Admn. Building
398 "B" Street
San Francisco, CA 94081

Milroy (Bud) Carnahan
Superintendent
Ligonier Valley School Dist.
120 E. Main Street
Ligonier, PA 15658

Ray Curran, Principal
Hudson Area High School
771 N. Maple Grove Ave.
Hudson, MI 49247

Michael Elsberry, Supt.
Struther City School Dist.
172 Sexton St.
Struther, OH 44471

Jerry L. Esplin, Principal
Malad High School
290 W. 400 N.
Malad City, ID 83252

Merrill Fellger
Director/K-12 Curriculum
ISD #877
Buffalo, MN

Aubrey Fillbrandt, Elem.
  Director
Windom Public Schools
Windom, MN 56101

Ferucio Freschet, Principal
Yorktown High School
2727 Compound Road
Yorktown Heights, NY
  10598

Ed D. Fauble, Principal
Pleasant View Elementary
  School
Pleasant Valley, IA 52767

Dr. Kenneth J. Grew,
  Superintendent
Grafton Public Schools
Grafton, MA 01519

Sue Greaves, MSW
White Bear Lake School
  District
3375 Willow Ave.
White Bear Lake, MN 55110

John Greupner
Ridgemount Jr. High
12000 Ridgemount Ave.
Plymouth, MN 55441

Kenneth N. Hanson,
  Principal
Montevideo Middle School
Third and Eureka
Montevideo, MN

Dr. Owen M. Henson,
  Assoc. Supt./Ed. Services
Topeka Public Schools
624 W. 24th St.
Topeka, KS 66611

Dr. Michael J. Homes
Plymouth-Canton
  Community Schools
454 S. Harvey
Plymouth, MI 48170

C. C. Kesl
Associate Principal
St. Anthony Village H.S.
3303-33rd Ave. NE
Minneapolis, MN 55418

Dr. Luther L. Kiser
Assistant Superintendent
Ames Community Schools
120 S. Kellogg
Ames, IA 50010

Dr. Carl S. Knox, Supt.
Lawrence Unified Schools
2017 Louisiana St.
Lawrence, KS 66044

Vincent LaCascio, Principal
Community School 102
1827 Archer St.
Bronx, NY 10460

Vern Lueth, Superintendent
Grand Marais, MN

R. Lorence, Principal
Mora Sr. High School
400 E. Maple Ave.
Mora, MN 55051

Martin Lynch
S. Washington County
  Schools
8040-80th St. S.
Cottage Grove, MN 55016

Dr. Marvin Maire, Supt.
Cedar Rapids, Community
  Schools
346 Second Ave. SW
Cedar Rapids, IA 52404

David C. Michaud, Principal
Stratham Memorial School
Bunker Hill Ave.
Stratham, NH 03885

Ron Mitchell, Principal
Sandburg Middle School
1902 Second Ave.
Anoka, MN 55303

Dr. John S. Marshall
Asst. Superintendent/Ed.
  Services
Oxnard School District
Oxnard, CA 93039

Vern L. Martin
Asst. Dir./Elem. Schools
Aurora Public Schools
1085 Peoria St.
Aurora, CO 80011

Jacqueline J. Moore,
  Principal
Mark Twain Elem. School
6316 Constitution NE
Albuquerque, NM

Dr. John H. Mosley,
  Superintendent
Ozark City Schools
Ozark, AL 36360

Ken Mumm, Asst. Principal
Kearney Jr. High
Kearney, NB 68847

Burt Nypen,
  Superintendent
Ortonville Public Schools
200-6th St. NW
Box 638
Ortonville, MN 56278

Milt Ojala
ISD #279
317 Second Ave. NW
Osseo, MN

Wm. Overman, Asst.
  Principal
Columbus Jr. High
1661-25th Ave.
Columbus, NB

Kenneth Pederson, Asst.
    Supt.
ISD #834
1875 S. Greeley
Stillwater, MN 55082

John Phipps
Cudahy Public Schools
3744 E. Ramsey Ave.
Cudahy, WI 53110

Dean Ray
Elementary Principal
Wichita Public Schools
Wichita, KS

Helen G. Renzi, Dir./
    Instruction
Williamstown Public Schools
96 School St.
Williamstown, MA 04267

Don Sherratt
Woodstock School
1900 Third St.
Alameda, CA 94501

Dr. Dick St. Germain
Dir./Secondary Ed.
N. St. Paul-Maplewood
    Schools
2055 E. Larpenteur Ave.
Maplewood, MN 55109

Robert J. Schaefer, Principal
Heim Middle School
175 Heim Road
Williamsville, NY 14221

Frederick N. Schwenk,
    Principal
Pennridge South Jr. High
    School
5th and Cedar St.
Perkasie, PA 18944

Alton O. Smedstad,
    Superintendent
Hillsboro Elementary
    Schools
512 NE Third
Hillsboro, OR 97123

T. S. Skaaland, Principal
Perham High School
Perham, MN

Dr. Les Sonnabend, Asst.
    Supt.
Prior Lake Public Schools
Prior Lake, MN

Don Swift, Dir./Pupil
    Services
Lorain City Schools
1020 Seventh St.
Lorain, OH 44052

Jerry Thompson
Elementary Principal
Frazee-Vergas Schools
Frazee, MN 56544

Dr. Jerome Warmus
Elementary Admn.
River Valley School Dist.
Spring Green, WI 53588

Roger B. Worner
Asst. Supt./Sec. Ed.
ISD #624
3375 Willow Ave.
White Bear Lake, MN 55110

Elwin Wright, Principal
Cedar Way Elementary
    School
22222-39th Ave. W.
Mountlake Terrace, WA
    98043

In addition to the variety of human resources available to aid school personnel in handling behavior problems, a growing body of professional literature offers teachers and administrators a rich array of helpful research, advice, and practical discipline strategies. The following section contains a selected bibliography of such contemporary references that have proved helpful to thousands of practicing professionals.

A TESTED BIBLIOGRAPHY ON BEHAVIOR

The books and articles below represent a gold mine of teacher-tested discipline theories and approaches with real-world applications appropriate for any school. These references can often serve as the catalyst for productive staff workshops and informal discussion groups aimed at bettering classroom and schoolwide behavior management.

Selected References on Discipline

"A Hard-Nosed Principal's Hard-Nosed Advice on School Discipline," *American School Board Journal,* 165, 4, 34-35, 56 April, 1978.

Clarizio, Harvey, F., *Toward Positive Classroom Discipline.* New York: John Wiley and Sons, 1971.

Curwin, Richard and Mendler, Allen. *The Discipline Book: A Complete Guide for School and Classroom Management.* Reston, VA: Reston Pub. Co., Inc., 1979.

Dinkmeyer, Don and Dinkmeyer, Don Jr. "Logical Consequences: A Key to the Reduction of Disciplinary Problems." *Phi Delta Kappan,* 57, 10 June 1976, pp. 664-666.

Discipline Crisis in Schools: The Problem, Causes, and the Search for Solutions. Arlington, VA: National School Public Relations Assoc., 1975.

Discipline—What Can Schools Do to Ensure It. Reston, VA: National Assoc. of Secondary School Principals, Feb., 1976.

Disruption in Urban Public Secondary Schools. Reston, VA: National Assoc. of Secondary School Principals, Feb., 1971.

Disruptive Youth: Causes and Solutions. Reston, VA: National Assoc. of Secondary School Principals, 1977.

Fagen, Stanley A., and Long, Nicholas J. "Before It Happens: Prevent Discipline Problems by Teaching Self-Control." *Instructor*, 85, 5 (January 1976) pp. 42-47, 95-96.

Glasser, William, *Reality Therapy*. New York: Harper & Row, 1972.

Got Discipline Problems? Do Something About Them. University of Tulsa, Tulsa, OK: Cadre, Allied Printers.

Howard, Eugene R. *School Discipline Desk Book*, West Nyack, NY: Parker Publishing Co., Inc., 1978.

Kindsvatter, Richard, and Levine, Mary Ann. "The Myth of Discipline," *Phi Delta Kappan*, Bloomington, IN, June 1980, pp. 690-698.

Methods of Discipline: What Is Allowed? Reston, VA: National Assoc. of Secondary School Principals, May 1976.

Orderly Schools That Serve All Children. Citizens Council for Ohio Schools, 517 The Arcade, Cleveland, Ohio 44114.

Partners: Parents and Schooling. Arlington, VA: Assoc. for Supervision and Curriculum Development, 1979.

Reutter, E. Edmund, Jr., "Liability in Student Discipline Cases," *IAR Research Bulletin* 15, 4, 1, 8-9 May 1975.

School Security: Guidelines for Maintaining Safety in School Desegregation. Washington, D.C.: U. S. Printing Office, 1979.

School Violence and Vandalism. Reston, VA: National Association of Secondary School Principals, 1975.

Search and Seizure in the Schools. Reston, VA: National Association of Secondary School Principals, February, 1979.

Shepardson, Richard D. *Elementary Teachers' Discipline Desk Book*. West Nyack, NY: Parker Publishing Co. Inc., 1980.

Student Discipline: Practical Approaches, NSBA Research Report 1979-2, National School Board Assoc., Washington, D.C., 1979.

"The Confidentiality of Pupil School Records," *A Legal Memorandum*. Reston, VA: National Secondary School Principals Assoc., September, 1976.

Violent Schools—Safe Schools. Washington D.C.: National Institute of Education, February, 1978.

By following the wealth of suggestions contained in this handbook and by utilizing the multitude of available resources described above, *positive school discipline is within the reach of every school.* The final section of this concluding chapter sums up the new view of discipline advocated throughout the handbook as the most effective, lasting approach to school harmony and productivity.

THE NEW VIEW: A HOLISTIC APPROACH TO DISCIPLINE

If public education is to fulfill society's promise to each individual learner and achieve the collective purposes of the school and the community, discipline must be positive and permanent. Modern times call for a new perspective of discipline as much more than security and safeguards or rewards and punishment.

From this broader view, effective discipline must be all of the following:

- An attitude (state of mind) that permeates the entire institution.
- An absolute requirement for achieving the school's goals.
- A way of life in the school.
- A collaborative endeavor.
- An avenue for directing energies and enthusiasm toward self-actualizing outcomes.
- A special kind of caring and respect for others.
- An integral part of the school's sense of unity and identity.
- A process and a product of learning.
- A handle on how to fix the "people things" that go wrong in schools.
- A foundation for maximum morale among students and adults in the school.
- A growth (learning) experience for all parties involved.

Discipline is at the heart of what schools are all about. It constitutes, in many ways, the only enduring curriculum. Positive discipline is both the goal and the daily life blood of the school. Its attainment requires the efforts of an active, continuing coalition among teachers, students, administrators, parents, and the community-at-large.

The emerging view of discipline parallels the broadened vision that characterizes modern health-care services. Today's medical community is moving rapidly beyond the limited treatment of symptoms and the correction of disorders toward an expanded emphasis on prevention, fitness, and maximum well-being. Likewise, the complex culture of today's school requires a well-rounded concept of discipline that is proactive and preventive.

Traditional school discipline has focused on punishing offenders and establishing docility among students. This approach, alone, is no longer effective or appropriate. The new thrust of discipline should be on moving beyond some precarious balance point between order and disorder and toward the ultimate goals of integrated growth and positive self-direction. This holistic view of and approach to school discipline is depicted in the continuum illustrated below.

DISCIPLINE CONTINUUM

Deterioration of Behavior ←

— Intergrated Growth →

Disruption/ Disorder

Positive, Self-directed Behavior

— Punishment System→ — Holistic Discipline →

○
Behavioral Balance Point

To achieve proper behavior and an optimum teaching/learning/working climate, school personnel must concentrate on the total spectrum of behavior represented by *both* sides of the continuum. The holistic approach requires that everyone in the school community learn together how to emphasize, encourage, and experience positive behavior, while reducing the time and attention devoted to punishment and negative control.

Good discipline marks the difference between a successful school and a school destined for failure and futility. The successful school in the 80's will find it increasingly necessary to adopt a holistic concept of school discipline and behavior management.

The ideas and suggestions in this handbook have been designed to flesh out this concept, to provide educators with tested tools for implementing it, and to help professionals shape schools that work and are something special in the learning lives of all students.

INDEX

DATE DUE